HEAVEN ON EARTH

Praise for *Heaven on Earth*

"*Heaven on Earth* helps us get past the idea that Christians are living for something that will be real after we die. I suggest we consider replacing 'Are you ready to die?' with 'Are you ready to live?'"
—Rubel Shelly, president of Rochester College (MI) and author of *I Knew Jesus Before He Was a Christian*

"Chris and Josh have unpacked the Sermon on the Mount in such a way that anyone can open this book to encounter first-century words with twenty-first-century eyes and close it having seen a glimpse of the kingdom of heaven."
—Dave Stone, senior pastor of Southeast Christian Church and author of the *Faithful Families* series

"A must read for those of us that want to better understand the true teachings of the Sermon on the Mount. Josh and Chris deliver a compelling read, drenched in years of study and experience . . . read this now!"
—Rob Thomas, president of Igniter Media and Graceway Media

"*Heaven On Earth* is a prophetic word inviting believers and curious bystanders to reengage the gospel of Jesus Christ as good news for the world here and now. This reminder that heaven is invading earth, and that we are invited to usher in its arrival, has never seemed more timely."
—Lauren Smelser White, Ph.D. candidate in Theological Studies, Vanderbilt University

"Chris Seidman and Joshua Graves have written a brilliant book that dives into the most important words ever spoken in the history of the world—the Beatitudes in Christ's preeminent Sermon on the Mount. It's no coincidence that the first word in the Beatitudes is the word "blessed." Reading *Heaven on Earth* you will learn that experiencing a blessed life is truly possible."
—Dudley Rutherford, author of *God Has an App for That!*

"Most of us are consistently asking ourselves, 'What does it mean to have the blessing of God? What does it mean to live the good life?' If you are looking for a taste of heaven on earth, if you'd like to see the kingdom of God come in your own life, then this book is a great place to start."
—Jonathan Storment, minister for Highland Church of Christ

REALIZING THE GOOD LIFE NOW

HEAVEN ON EARTH

CHRIS SEIDMAN & JOSHUA GRAVES

ABINGDON PRESS *Nashville*

HEAVEN ON EARTH
REALIZING THE GOOD LIFE NOW

Library of Congress Cataloging-in-Publication Data

Seidman, Chris.
    Heaven on earth : realizing the good life now / Chris Seidman & Joshua Graves.
       p. cm.
    Includes bibliographical references and index.
    ISBN 978-1-4267-4904-9 (pbk. : alk. paper) 1. Christian life. 2. Beatitudes. I. Graves, Joshua, 1979- II. Title.
    BV4501.3.S445 2012
    241.5'3--dc23
                                                                    2012038370

12 13 14 15 16 17 18 19 20 21—10 9 8 7 6 5 4 3 2 1
MANUFACTURED IN THE UNITED STATES OF AMERICA

For Lucas and Finn Graves
For Skyler, Garrison, and Cooper Seidman

Like arrows in the hands of a warrior
   are children born in one's youth . . .
They will not be put to shame,
   when they contend with their opponents in court.
                    —Psalm 127:4–5

For our sons—God is closer to you than the blood in your veins.

CONTENTS

HEAVEN ON EARTH
realizing the good life now

Every so often we hear of fighter pilots engaged in high-speed maneuvers who, tragically, fly straight into the ground or ocean. Sometimes the accident occurs because of a malfunction of the plane's computerized operating system or a mechanical breakdown of some kind. But there is also the possibility that the pilot had become disoriented, if only for a few brief moments, and flown by instinct, instead of the instrument panel. Sometimes pilots travel so fast and engage in so many different maneuvers that they lose their sense of orientation and no longer know which way is really "up." This can prove to be disastrous when the pilots turn the controls in what they think will help them ascend into the sky, only to descend straight into the ground.

Many of us are flying full-throttle through our lives. We live at a speed that borders on breaking the sound barrier, thinking we think we know which way is "up"—what we need to do to "ascend." In many cases, we fly straight into the ground. There are times when we're flying upside down and don't even know it. This is a book about getting our bearings and truly discerning which way is really "up" when it comes to knowing what "the good life" is.

North Americans are consumed with a desire to experience the good life. Savvy advertisers spend billions of dollars painting pictures of what the good life is and how their product is an integral part of it. The entertainment industry spins its own narratives embodying the good life. Entire magazines and websites are radically devoted to capturing the essence of the good life. But what really is the good life, and how do we stay on course? How do we avoid crashing? Beyond that, what is the flight mission in the first place? The "good life" spoken of in the pages that follow refers not to a particular standard of living but to a quality of life—a beautiful and effective life—a life that makes a difference. So where do we begin?

GETTING OUR BEARINGS

The very first word in Jesus' very first sermon recorded in Scripture is the word *blessed* (Matthew 5:3). The fact that Jesus uses this word to begin his sermon, as opposed to *cursed*, tells us much about the heart of God. *Blessed* is a multilayered word and we will turn our attention to it again later in the book. For now, though, one of the things *blessed* implies is this—we've been made privileged or fortunate by the action of someone beyond us.

Being blessed is different than getting lucky. Luck implies happenstance—as in we "just happened" across something good. But in "being blessed" we're referring to a state of fortune or favor we find ourselves in because of the presence and activity of someone else in our lives.

Jesus once said, "No one is good—except God alone" (Mark 10:18). The good life is only possible in so far as God is involved. Experiencing the good life is more about what God has done and is doing than what we have done or are doing. Finding the good life is only possible to the degree that we allow our lives to be swallowed up in God's life.

NOT PRESCRIPTIONS BUT DESCRIPTIONS

Jesus' opening words in the Sermon on the Mount in Matthew 5:3–12, most commonly referred to as the Beatitudes, are navigational beacons that tell us where the good life is found, because they tell us where *God* is found. And where God is found is where the potential for heavenly realities will be experienced—heaven on earth.

The Beatitudes are not prescriptions for us to follow in order to gain divine favor from above that blesses our own ambitions and plans. The Beatitudes are descriptions of where God is found, who God is blessing, and what a difference God's kingdom breaking into the world makes.

In the very first chapter we'll explore what on earth the "kingdom of heaven" meant in Jesus' day and what it means for our world today. The kingdom of heaven coming near through Jesus makes a difference.

The kingdom of heaven makes a difference for the poor in spirit—those who are in a broken condition far beyond their own capacity and resources to repair.

It makes a difference for those who mourn—those who are acutely aware of and grieved by the world as it is; and how far removed it is from what God intended for it to be all along.

It makes a difference for the meek—those who are "small" and surrendered to God out of a profound sense of their "smallness."

It makes a difference for those who hunger and thirst for righteousness—those who crave for things to be made right again in their lives and world.

It makes a difference for the merciful—those who are generous in deeds of deliverance on behalf of others in bondage to guilt and need.

It makes a difference for the pure in heart—those whose desire (even desperation) for God is undiluted.

It makes a difference for the peacemakers—those who are contending for God's wholeness—God's shalom—in our violent, fragmented world.

It makes a difference for those who are persecuted because of righteousness—for those who are done wrong precisely because they are doing right.

As we align our lives with these realities, we become as salt and light in the world—difference-makers. But we are only as salty and enlightening in our world to the degree that we reflect the nature of the King and his kingdom as described in the Beatitudes.

The Beatitudes offer us a way to get our bearings as to where God is, what difference God's kingdom makes, and invite us to align our lives accordingly. They give us hope when we find ourselves in the shoes of those the Beatitudes describe. They give us direction when we find ourselves longing to be where God is and doing what God is doing.

This book was birthed out of a year's worth of dialogue between us (Josh and Chris) as we personally wrestled with and explored the Sermon on the Mount in our respective churches. We do not profess to know the full meaning nor complete implications of the Beatitudes, and we have yet to be living completely in light of them. We very much see ourselves in light of the apostle Paul's words when speaking of a day to come, "Now I know in part; then I shall know fully, even as I am fully known" (1 Corinthians 13:12). We see dimly, but it is our hope that our reflections will serve as worthwhile conversation partners for you on a journey to more fully realize heaven on earth—not just for your sake but for the sake of the world around you.

HEAVEN HAPPENS

*"The kingdom of heaven
has come near."
(Matthew 4:17)*

When we marry into a family, go off to college, move to a different part of the country, or join a church, we discover there are words and expressions used in the family, college, region, or church that mean something to that particular community. Every word or expression has a story behind it, and if we don't know the story, the assumptions we make or conclusions we reach may range from comical, to confusing, to even harmful.

Context is so important. This is particularly true when it comes to understanding what Jesus was saying in the Beatitudes. In order to fully grasp the Beatitudes, we need a sense of their context. These declarations were made on the heels of a declaration Jesus made about the kingdom of heaven as well as a demonstration of its power. Having a

1

sense of where Jesus was and what he was saying and doing just prior to the Beatitudes helps us better understand them and apply them to our own context in life.

THE KINGDOM OF HEAVEN

Fred Smith was an influential businessman who mentored Christian leaders for several decades through Leadership Network. In the summer of 2004, he was hospitalized and not expected to live. Family members heard him repeat, "I want to go home . . . I want to go home." After a family meeting of great angst, they decided to respect his wishes, removing him from dialysis, knowing that his death would come in three to five days. For the next thirty-six hours, they sang, read Scripture, prayed, and said their goodbyes. But unexpectedly, the anticipated peaceful decline was anything but. Fred went into pulmonary failure and choking aspiration. His daughter, Brenda, sat with him through the difficult night. The coughing, however, stirred Fred out of his semiconscious state and he fully awoke. Brenda quietly told him of the family's decision to follow his desire to go home. She explained that he would slip into unconsciousness and then step from here to there.

Suddenly Fred's eyes were wide open and he made the effort to speak: "Home? I didn't mean heaven, I meant Parkchester" (his house on Parkchester Drive). Laughing through her tears, Brenda quickly called for the doctors. His dialysis was rescheduled and Fred recovered to go home and live three more years. For Fred, *home* was more than a place on the other side of the grave. Home was also on Parkchester Drive.[1] Context is everything. Fred was talking about his life *on this side* of the grave when he used the word *home* while his family was thinking of home as a reference to his life on *the other side* of the grave.

This same thing happens with many of us in understanding Jesus' words about "the kingdom of heaven." For Jesus, the kingdom of heaven had everything to do with life on this side of the grave while many of us are inclined to think it mostly has something to do with life on the other side. Consequently, we think of Jesus' proclamation of the kingdom of heaven coming near as meaning through Jesus we now have access to the place of heaven after we die. Even though this is one aspect of the context, it is not the entire context.

While Jesus is the Way to life beyond the grave, what Jesus was referring to when he spoke of the kingdom of heaven coming near, and what his original audience would have pictured when they heard him proclaim that the kingdom of heaven coming near, was more immediate.

Jesus' listeners were brought up reading the prophet Isaiah's proclamations about the kingdom of God (the phrases "kingdom of God" and "kingdom of heaven" are synonymous). Isaiah described the kingdom of God not so much as a realm beyond the grave, but as the sphere of God's reign, rule, activity, and work upon the earth.

In Isaiah's prophecies, "kingdom of God" doesn't refer exclusively to a place beyond the grave, but a "happening" upon the earth. In

Matthew's Gospel, Jesus comes on the scene declaring that the reign, the rule, the activity of God—"the kingdom of heaven"—is near. The kingdom of heaven is *happening*.

WHEN HEAVEN HAPPENS

And when heaven "is happening" on the earth, lives are changed. Seventeen passages in Isaiah speak of the kingdom of God and all seventeen of them speak of it in terms of one thing: deliverance or salvation.[2] This makes the meaning of Jesus' name all the more significant: "the Lord saves" (Matthew 1:21). Jesus' name is inextricably intertwined with what the kingdom of God represents. The saving, delivering, rule, reign, activity of God comes near in the life, ministry, message, and presence of Jesus upon the earth. Isaiah fleshes out what this deliverance and salvation means, very specifically. Salvation is described in terms of *peace* (14 times); *healing* (7 times); *joy* (12 times); *return from estrangement with God* (9 times); and *righteousness, justice, fairness* (16 times).[3]

When Jesus echoes Isaiah's language about the kingdom of heaven, he's referring to the saving, delivering, rule, reign, and power of God on the earth that makes a qualitative difference in people's lives on the earth. In Jesus' saving reign, people would experience peace, healing, joy, a newfound sense of restoration with God, and an atmosphere of righteousness and justice.

SHOW AND TELL

Jesus didn't just declare that the kingdom of heaven was near. He demonstrated it as well. He was into "show and tell."

> Jesus went throughout Galilee, teaching in their synagogues, proclaiming the good news of the kingdom, and healing every disease and sickness among the people. News about him spread all over Syria, and people brought to him all who were ill with various diseases, those suffering severe pain, the demon-possessed, those having seizures, and the paralyzed; and he healed them. Large crowds from Galilee, the Decapolis, Jerusalem, Judea and the region across the Jordan followed him. (Matthew 4:23–25)

This is the story immediately preceding Jesus going up on a mountainside to give what came to be known as the Sermon on the Mount (Matthew 5—7), which begins with the words of the Beatitudes. But before he spoke from the mountain, he delivered people in their valleys. In the Beatitudes and the Sermon on the Mount, Jesus tells his followers about the nature of the King and what it means to live in light of the reign of God on the earth. And he gives listeners a living picture of the kingdom. He heals people: the aged and infirm, the fevered and the paralyzed, the mentally anguished, the epileptics, the afflicted—he healed them all.

HEALING MORE THAN MEETS THE EYE

So suppose you lived in Palestine, in the area of Galilee, in the days of Jesus and were chronically ill. In addition to suffering the

5

adversity of the illness itself, you also would have endured a ripple effect of related consequences.

There were economic consequences because there was no welfare plan or social security for you. You couldn't work due to illness and were in real trouble because there were no "safety nets." You lived day-to-day under the crippling weight of taxation in the Roman Empire. It didn't take you long to slip into the quicksand of debt at a pace where you would probably never catch up. You were so sunk financially that your primary option for survival was begging.[4]

And you're alone. In the days of Jesus, people didn't just withdraw from you—*they isolated you*—trying to manage the disease, minimizing the opportunity for it to spread. But the isolation was also spiritualized: many suspected your sickness was a clue that you were under the judgment of God for your sins, or even the sins of your parents (see John 9:1–2).

You're chronically ill. Bankrupt. Isolated from society, and (to top it all off) told that God turned his back on you because of something you or your parents had done (again, see John 9:1–2).

Do the math and the sum total is a profound sense of brokenness, powerlessness, despair. A broken body and mind, but also a broken spirit.

Then Jesus appears on the scene, declaring the kingdom of heaven is near and healing all who were brought to him, including you. When Jesus healed you, he not only freed you from your suffering, but set processes in motion for you to return to society again; to be in relationships; to have the opportunity to work again and not be in a position to grapple with the shame of begging; and, the most significant healing of all, having your perceptions corrected about God having distanced himself from you. Imagine the kind of joy you would experience in the wake of being healed. *Blessed (makarioi,* also translated as *joyful)* is the description Jesus used for this experience of the kingdom of heaven upon the earth. The blessing that is the kingdom of heaven had *real life* implications: bodies healed, relationships restored, dignity renewed, false assumptions about God shattered. Jesus declaring the kingdom of heaven is near wasn't just something figurative, symbolic, or "internally spiritual." *The kingdom of heaven coming near was making a difference in the quality of people's lives.*

A FUNNY THING ABOUT THESE WALLS

Perhaps you're thinking, *Thanks for the history lesson.* But this isn't about ancient history, this is about "the here and now" and the future. Jesus' life and teachings aren't recorded to tell us who he was and what he did, but who he is and what he's doing. Heaven is happening today.

The Academy Award-winning movie *The Shawshank Redemption* tells the story of life in a maximum security prison for perpetrators of violent crimes. In the movie we meet up with Brooks (played by James Whitmore), who began serving a life sentence for murder in 1905.

Now, fifty years later, he came up for parole and was approved for release. Learning of his approved release, Brooks promptly attempted to kill a fellow prison inmate—a friend, in fact. The other inmates and guards intervened and prevented him from doing so. Brooks broke down and wept like a baby. The guards never reported the incident. Reluctantly, Brooks left Shawshank Penitentiary to live in a halfway house and begin his new life in the free world.

Later, as Brooks's fellow inmates sat on bleachers overlooking the recreation area inside the penitentiary, they confessed to one another how baffled they were at Brooks's actions. For fifty years he'd been a peaceful and compliant man behind bars, yet the very moment he was approved for release he attempted to do something that would keep him behind bars for good. Red (played by Morgan Freeman), the resident sage among the inmates who himself was behind bars for a violent crime, offered this response, "It's a funny thing about these prison walls. At first you hate them. Then you get used to them. Then you grow to depend on them. Brooks was an institutionalized man."

Institutionalization isn't just something imagined in the movies. It happens in the real world. Sometimes a person can be in one condition for so long, surrounded by the same set of circumstances for so long, that it becomes "normal" to them. They can't imagine life without their walls. Perhaps this is why Jesus, on one occasion, asked a man who had been lame for almost four decades if he wanted to be healed (see John 5:6).

Many of us know what it is to be "walled in" in our lives by an awareness of our brokenness. If we live long enough with such an awareness and void of hope of things being any different, I suppose it's possible for us to transition from hating our walls, to getting used to our walls, to even depending on our walls. But according to God's track record in Scripture, he's been known to tear down walls—of all kinds. In the midst of a world of institutionalization, God brings about transformation. This is what the kingdom of heaven is about.

One of the things Jesus would later teach his disciples to pray for was for things to be on earth as they are in heaven (Matthew 6:10). In heaven tears are wiped away; there is no poverty, sickness, suffering, addiction, bondage, division, hatred, racism, oppression, sin, guilt, or shame. In calling us to pray for things to be on earth as they are in heaven, Jesus is calling us to join his movement, prayerfully contending for the transformation of our lives and our world and refusing to yield to a spirit of institutionalization. We see heaven happen when we witness moments where a poverty-based need is met, sickness healed, suffering alleviated, sobriety settles in, justice established, equality affirmed, or sins forgiven.

MAKING THE ASCENT

After a demonstration of healings, Jesus ascends the mountainside and pronounces blessing.

> Now when Jesus saw the crowds, he went up on a mountainside and
> sat down. His disciples came to him, and he began to teach them. He
> said, "Blessed are the poor in spirit, for theirs is the kingdom of heaven."
> (Matthew 5:1–3)

The Beatitudes are Jesus' commentary on all that his disciples have
been witnessing and will witness by Jesus' side in the future. They are
his "inauguration speech," in which he is articulating the values of the
King and how God administrates his kingdom because God longs for us
to align our lives accordingly. Matthew says that "his disciples came to
him." Here's the picture of a disciple—one who comes out of the crowd
and makes the ascent to be with Jesus. But every ascent to be with
Jesus is for the purpose of making another *descent*—going down from
the mountain to live in the valleys of brokenness as conduits through
which the kingdom of heaven happens.

HOME

For Fred Smith, "home" wasn't just heaven. It was also on this side
of the grave, on Parkchester Drive. For Jesus, the "kingdom of heaven"
is also on this side of the grave. As well the well-known pastor and
writer Frederick Buechner notes:

> If we only had eyes to see and ears to hear and wits to understand,
> we would know that the Kingdom of God in the sense of holiness, good-
> ness, beauty is as close as breathing and is crying out to be born within
> ourselves and within the world; we would know that the Kingdom of God

is what all of us hunger for above all other things even when we don't know its name or realize that it's what we're starving to death for. The Kingdom of God is where our best dreams come from and our truest prayers. We glimpse it at those moments when we find ourselves being better than we are and wiser than we know. We catch sight of it when at some moment of crisis a strength seems to come to us that [is] greater than our own strength. The Kingdom of God is where we belong. It is home, and whether we realize it or not, I think we are all of us homesick for it.[5]

What Buechner refers to as "home" is not limited to a reality found on the other side of the grave. It is something we taste on this side of the grave. Through Jesus the kingdom of heaven happens. It's closer than we think and more accessible than we realize.

It's where we belong.

And it's time to go home.

FOR THE BANKRUPT

CHAPTER 2
CHRIS

"Blessed are the poor in spirit,
for theirs is the kingdom
of heaven."
(Matthew 5:3)

For much of the summer of 2010, we helplessly watched our oldest child lie motionless in hospital isolation for weeks, his body battling bacterial meningitis, and later MRSA (a staph infection resistant to most antibiotics). We were painfully aware that Skyler's body did not have enough resources to contend with what was trying to kill him. Infectious disease doctors themselves acknowledged the limitations of their own resources to help him. Thankfully, Skyler was spared. Today, our thirteen-year-old has a peculiar awareness, for his age, of his own mortality, vulnerability, and limited resources.

My father-in-law had this awareness as well. At the age of thirty-two, within three weeks of being diagnosed with multiple sclerosis, he was in a wheelchair. For the last seventeen years of his life, he lived with the disease gradually stripping him of his capacity to do simple daily routines that many of us take for granted. He taught me much about living with a deeply rooted faith in the goodness of God in the midst of his suffering, all the while being acutely aware that he did not have enough resources, in and of himself, to conquer multiple sclerosis.

I have a grandfather who was a lifelong entrepreneur who went broke three different times in his life, another family member who's battled depression since he was a small child, a dear friend who has been an alcoholic for more than thirty years and is celebrating four years of sobriety. And then, of course, there is my own reflection in the mirror every morning.

Sooner or later, we face brokenness in our lives and world that far exceeds the resources we have, in and of ourselves, to address and repair the brokenness. It could be a struggle with an illness, depression or addiction of some kind; a financial disaster; or the end of a relationship. All kinds of life experiences can usher us into a profound awareness of our own bankruptcy—be it physical, mental, financial, emotional, or spiritual. Few things are more disheartening than the realization that we don't have "what it takes" to make ourselves (or ones we love) whole; or to meet a challenge; fulfill an obligation; live up to a standard. The writer of Proverbs had something to say about the crippling weight of a broken spirit: "The human spirit can endure in sickness, / but a *crushed spirit* who can bear?" (Proverbs 18:14, emphasis added).

The psalmist, though, reminds us, "The LORD is close to the brokenhearted / and saves those who are *crushed in spirit*" (Psalm 34:18, emphasis added). For all those who are disheartened by a sense of their own bankruptcy, Jesus makes a liberating declaration.

GOD HELPS THOSE WHO CANNOT HELP THEMSELVES

When Jesus says, "Blessed are the poor in spirit, for theirs is the kingdom of heaven," his words erupt out of a vivid context and experience of his healing and transforming lives. He is not giving a prescription for how one should live in order to "get blessed." (Some readers have taken it to be just that—as though one must "become" poor in spirit in order to possess the kingdom of heaven. But we already are "poor in spirit" without even trying—more about that later.) On the contrary, Jesus is making a declaration of the way things are in light of the kingdom of heaven that is breaking forth in his very body. He's recognizing the ones to whom the kingdom of heaven belongs. The kingdom of heaven is for the poor in spirit. Therefore, it's the poor in spirit who are "blessed" or "joyful" because the kingdom of heaven belongs to them. The reigning, ruling, saving, delivering power of God is breaking into the world— not against them, but for them! Through Jesus, God has come to help those who cannot help themselves—who are broken beyond their own ability and resources to repair their lives.

15

GRACE FOR US

The good news is the kingdom of heaven belongs to the poor in spirit, and the sobering news is this is what we are. One doesn't have to "become" poor in spirit because that is what all of us are. Jesus doesn't say the kingdom of heaven belongs to those who "realize" they are poor in spirit. He says it belongs to the poor in spirit. This is a promise for all of us, but it only makes a difference for each of us to the degree that we awaken to the reality of our poverty of spirit and the wonder of the kingdom promised.

The apostle Paul put it this way, "There is no one righteous, not even one; . . . for all have sinned and fall short of the glory of God" (Romans 3:10, 23). What is curious is that it seems the longer one walks with God, the more aware they become of their poverty of spirit. It's interesting to note this progression of awareness in the apostle Paul's own life. In one of his earliest letters, he referred to himself as the "least of the apostles" (1 Corinthians 15:9). A few years later, he referred to himself as the "least of all the Lord's people" (Ephesians 3:8). Still, even years later in one of his last letters, he referred to himself as the "worst of sinners" (1 Timothy 1:16). The longer Paul dwelled in the kingdom of light the more aware he became of the darkness in his own life.

I think about the evolution of Paul's awareness of his own spiritual poverty in contrast to the results of a survey conducted several years ago of over a million high school students that asked them how well they got along with their peers. Sixty percent of the students believed they were in the top 10 percent of how well they got along with their peers. Twenty-five percent of the students believed they were in the top 1 percent. One might think college professors would have more self-awareness, but they didn't. When the same survey was done, 63 percent of them thought they were above average and 25 percent of them rated themselves as truly exceptional when it came to how well they got along with their peers. One researcher assessed the survey's findings and commented, "The average person believes he is a better person than the average person." Psychologists have a name for this. It's called "illusory superiority." We tend to think better of ourselves than we really are.[1]

There are many reasons that we tend to think we are better than we are, but in doing so we drift further from reality. Reality is found in Christ (see Colossians 2:17). His coming tells us much about our true condition. He came to bring that which we could not access on our own effort, power, or piety. This is why it is such liberating news that the kingdom of heaven *belongs* to the poor in spirit. The irony is in failing to acknowledge our own weaknesses—our own spiritual poverty—we alienate ourselves from the very power and grace that could transform our lives. The failure to name our poverty of spirit is, in a sense, an evasion of the very grace Jesus came to bring.

Tasting of heaven on earth is possible because of the gracious initiative of God through Jesus Christ. Some people think they've forfeited their opportunity to experience the good life because of decisions they've made in the past or even experiences they've had that have convinced them that God has distanced himself from them for the rest of their lives. Others are enslaved to the false idea they must live a good life in order to find grace at the end of their days before the judgment seat of God—as though they must "earn" grace. Jesus' declaration about the kingdom of heaven begs to differ. The foundational verse of the Beatitudes (and, for that matter, the entire Sermon on the Mount) is the declaration that the grace of God is present for all who are broken. The Beatitudes begin on the heels of a display of grace. Grace is the swaddling cloth of our lives. We are born into a broken world, and yet a world where the grace of the kingdom of heaven is present in the midst of such brokenness. It has been the experience of many that upon finally realizing their own brokenness they want to run from God. This has been true since the beginning of time (consider Adam and Eve's response to their brokenness). All the while, the God we're inclined to run from has drawn near to us in Jesus.

My friend Charlie Ulrich had been running from God most of his life. Charlie was a seventy-nine-year-old retired merchant marine who had worked hard, lived hard, and played hard while spending most of his life on the open seas all over the world. He was "weathered" in every sense of the word. Other than the occasional wedding or funeral, he didn't set foot inside a church much. A woman changed all that, though. Charlie was brought to church by his eighty-year-old girlfriend Willie Mae. He genuinely enjoyed his first several weeks at church. One Sunday, though, I ran into Charlie in the lobby and his disposition had changed. He was downcast. I asked him what was going on. He said,

"It's just hitting me that I don't belong here. I'm not like all these good, righteous people (he wasn't being sarcastic). I can understand why God would have something to do with them, but I don't see why he'd have anything to do with me!"

Charlie had yet to really believe and understand we were just as spiritually broken as he was—he just hadn't been around us long enough to know it—and that the kingdom of heaven belongs to the broken. Charlie stuck around long enough, though, for this reality to settle into his soul. Weeks later, I had the privilege of baptizing Charlie. When he turned eighty, Charlie told me he hadn't felt "this young in decades"—that knowing Jesus really had brought him life. If you knew Charlie in the last years of his life, he looked like he had won the lottery. In fact, that's how he often described his feelings about his newfound faith—like he had won the lottery. But it wasn't the lottery. He had awakened to the glorious truth that the kingdom of heaven was for him. Blessed is Charlie Ulrich, for his is the kingdom of heaven.

GRACE THROUGH US

Makarioi (blessed) is found fifty times throughout the New Testament and is most often used in reference to the joy of experiencing God's action of deliverance.[2] The blessedness of experiencing God's action of deliverance, though, isn't exclusively reserved for those on the receiving end of it, like Charlie. There's a blessedness to be experienced on the part of those who are channels for the delivering activity of the kingdom of heaven. Makarioi is not only found in Matthew 5:3–12, but also Acts 20:35: "It is more blessed to give than to receive." The grace of the kingdom is experienced not only in receiving but in giving. We were created in the image of the Giver. Jesus "fleshes out" such an image before our eyes and calls us to follow him in regard to the poor in spirit. We ascend the mountain with Jesus to take on his perspective, values, mind, agenda that we might become as he is. As God transforms our lives, we become conduits of God's saving, delivering power that makes a difference in the lives of others. In following God we find our true selves—what we were created to be all along—and, therein, experience blessedness—the Good Life.

Several years ago, a friend lost her sister in a tragic accident. The sister was with her children in a crowd watching a parade when a Nigerian man, newly arrived to America and on the heels of having lost his whole family in Nigeria, was driving through a small town way too fast. Somehow he wound up driving into the parade route and hit a parked car, flipping his car into the crowd. The woman had time to push her children out of the way, but was pinned in between a tree and the car. She died there while the driver lived. There's not a day that passes without my friend thinking of her sister, but recently told me she's experienced more healing in the last year over her loss than ever before. She attributes her healing to going to Ghana, the neighboring country to Nigeria, and serving orphans who were once child slaves. Her service to them isn't just in Ghana. It's also here in the states as well, as an advocate on their behalf. My friend has found healing in the blessedness of participating in God's deliverance of those who cannot help themselves.

John serves as a sponsor in AA. He moves among people who are broken beyond their own capacity to repair themselves. Out of his own mess, he brings a message of hope to those who live on the edge of hopelessness in regard to their addictions. John has found a measure of healing in the blessedness of participating in God's deliverance of those who cannot help themselves.

Linda is a woman in her mid-sixties whose child died four decades earlier. Just in the last few years she has made long strides in her healing through the experience of devoting herself to serving disadvantaged children and children with special needs. There's a blessedness to be experienced because of the kingdom of heaven coming to us in our brokenness and through us to others in their brokenness.

BEGINNING AT THE END OF OURSELVES

So where do we begin when it comes to living in light of Jesus' opening beatitude? We begin by coming to the end of ourselves—by acknowledging and confessing we are "in deep" and "over our heads" in brokenness when it comes to our standing before God and our resources to put ourselves and our world back together. And if we need any help coming to a fuller realization of our bankruptcy, soaking in the Sermon on the Mount will do just fine. Jesus' vision of what a righteous life looks like when it's lived from the heart outward can bring us to a realization that we don't have, in and of ourselves, this kind of righteousness. Living out Jesus' visionary teaching for our lives is predicated upon us realizing we cannot do it by ourselves. We are among the ones whom the kingdom of heaven is for—the spiritually bankrupt.

In the wake of such a confession, we experience the reality of God's grace and power in the midst of our own brokenness—grace and power that is not intended to stop with us, but to flow through us to others in their brokenness. Through coming to the end of ourselves we are actually liberated unto a life of moving beyond ourselves through service to others in their brokenness as we have been served in ours. Jesus would tell his disciples later, "Freely you have received; freely give" (Matthew 10:8). What is received is meant to be given. And it's in the giving we'll find ourselves receiving all the more. Grace upon grace.

*"Blessed are those who mourn,
for they will be comforted."
(Matthew 5:4)*

ACHING VISIONARIES

A MILLION PIECES

In *The Year of Magical Thinking*, Joan Didion describes the year her life fell apart. Didion's daughter fought for her own life after a horrible accident during which her husband died tragically and unexpectedly. Life was no longer beautiful, meaningful, or lovely.

Life was hell because everything went to pieces in an instant. "The ordinary instant."

Last year, several friends flew to Dallas/Fort Worth to attend the funeral of the sister of one of my best friends. She, in her early thirties, died of sepsis. Her younger brother led worship. At one point the entire room sang Leonard Cohen's "It's a cold and it's a broken hallelujah.

Hallelujah . . . Hallelujah." I awoke in the middle of the night before my early flight with this haunting song in my head. To hear them now leading the song with the casket in plain view was a profoundly spiritual moment. We also sang other spiritual songs of lament and pain.

Her oldest brother delivered the eulogy for his sister: "We're confident that death doesn't have the last word; death doesn't win." Before Rob Bell said it, her brother said it: *Love wins*. He confessed to the church that God had not answered their prayers the way they desired. He did not offer the unfortunate sound bites well-meaning Christians often offer: "God's ways are mysterious." "God needed another angel." "God has a plan."

Sentimentality does not help in times of crisis and loss. In fact, it often makes things worse. Perhaps the most powerful moment in the worship gathering occurred near the end of the eulogy. The young man addressed each person in his family:

To his parents: "You raised us to have faith in difficult situations. All you wanted to do was point us to Christ. She was your princess. She treasured you."

To his only brother: "We'll find a way. We will get through this."

To his brother-in-law: "We are family, no matter what. Thanks for loving my sister without conditions. You loved her unconditionally. We are so grateful for you. We're in this together with you for life."

To his niece: "We will fight for your faith. We will fight for you to know Jesus. Your mother wanted your faith to surpass her faith."

MOURNERS

Jesus' life was about bringing heaven to earth.

Jesus' life was about helping humanity realize the good life, the God-life, in the here and now not simply the "then and there."

And, sometimes, this is difficult. Not impossible. But difficult to see how Jesus accomplished such a task.

Jesus arrives on the scene, knowing the tragedy and death that had consumed the lives of the poor peasants in Israel and, with great courage declared that those in mourning would be comforted. At first glance, it seems a little trite. Kind of like telling someone who's just lost a loved one that "God needed another angel" or "God needed her more than you do."

But Jesus was not saying to his followers "One day it will all make sense." Jesus was saying, when you are in mourning God is with you. Perhaps some Jews in the first century (as is true of Christians in America today) had come to believe the first-century version of Joel Osteen's *Your Best Life Now*. That is, some believed that success was a sure sign of God's favor—it's one of the ways affluent folks control the poor. The poor, Jesus' original audience, had come to believe that their struggle, experience with death, disease, and sickness was a sign of God's judgment. Jesus says, "No, God isn't like that. God is among those who find themselves in tears." Because there's something to be said for a good cry. Let's break it down.

25

When Jesus addresses *mourning* he's describing something beyond weeping. The word normally translated into mourning is *penthountes*. It is more properly understood as being deeply saddened and grieved to the point of action.

Human beings weep over pretty much anything—a Nicolas Sparks novel, a movie, a football game (particularly if you grew up rooting for the Detroit Lions).

Mourning is something different. It refers to a deep sadness that's rooted in a profound loss. The kind of loss that can't ever be fixed. Crying is almost always a part of the mourning process but mourning isn't simply crying.

Some losses can't be undone, like the loss of a spouse, the disappearance of a child, the betrayal of a best friend. Mourning is about a grief that compels one to act.

Jesus' audience was full of people dealing with a profound sense of loss on many levels and they weren't going to be able to fix things on their own.

When Jesus stands up and says, *blessed are those who mourn, for they will be comforted,* Jesus is further investigating and teaching what he's just done; the manner in which he's brought heaven's future to earth's present. He doesn't simply talk about salvation, he embodies it.

This is heaven on earth.

There's a new kind of niche bar in Asia called a cry bar. A cry bar is a bar with some sofas, a few tables, and lots and lots of tissues where people can pay $6 an hour to come in, sit, and cry. Owner Luo Jun in the Chinese port city of Nanjing said he opened the bar when clients from a previous business confessed a desire to cry but didn't know when or where it would be appropriate to do so.[1]

How many bars in the United States fill the same purpose? People are gathering to mourn by staring down a bottle.

And they don't even know what's happening.

Numb. Mourning inside to the depths of their bones.

John was a missionary and scholar in Uganda (East Africa) for almost a decade. He describes authentic mourning in this way: "Women are especially expressive, depending on their relationships to the deceased; they will wail loudly and throw themselves on the ground. It can serve both as expression of pain and sorrow, and as community participation and even communication. I remember passing a home in a village one day at the precise moment when a sick baby died and I heard the mother let out her first wail. It was bloodcurdling. It also served as an announcement to those around. Everyone in the village immediately knew what had happened, and as I stood there, women started appearing out of every direction, walking toward the hut and joining a growing chorus of wails as the larger community started surrounding the young mother and processing the death together. It was remarkable."

Scholars remind us that the word for mourning in this passage means to be deeply moved to the point of action. Mourning doesn't simply mean "sad" or "depressed"—though those are real human emotions we need to pay attention to. Mourning rather means moved deeply in one's gut to see the world, through your tears, in a new way, longing for things to be different. Amos 6:1–7 describes it like this:

> Woe to you who are complacent in Zion. . . .
> You lie on beds adorned with ivory
>   and lounge on your couches.
> You dine on choice lambs
>   and fattened calves.
> You strum away on your harps like David
>   and improvise on musical instruments.
> You drink wine by the bowlful
>   and use the finest lotions,
>   *but you do not grieve over the ruin of Joseph.*
> Therefore you will be among the first to go into exile;
>   your feasting and lounging will end. (emphasis added)

Mourning is about a fire in your belly.

It means longing for lonely people in nursing homes to experience deep community.

It means hoping for the end of HIV/AIDS.

It means yearning for the end of the effects of famine.

It means having your guts ripped out for those orphans who have no hope.

Mourning is a pure vision of the large gulf between how things could *be* versus how things actually *are*.

As I was editing this chapter I received an e-mail from a friend describing a recent trip to Haiti in which he watched a mother smother

her newborn son because the orphanage he was working with had no more room to take in new children.

In broad daylight, in front of several people, she smothered her newborn while walking away from the orphanage workers in anger.

This is a messed-up world.

Mourning also means being moved in such a way that you intend to do something about it. It means summoning the courage to visit an assisted living facility even if it freaks you out. Mourning doesn't mean you are overly emotional, a cry-baby, or soft. Mourning means you have a deep awareness of just how messed up things really are from the way things should be. In mourning, you are as close to God as you'll ever be. One prominent theologian, who lost his son in a horrible hiking accident, says that mourners are "aching visionaries."[2]

William Wilberforce believed England was obligated to end slavery and he dedicated his entire life to see that happen. Mother Teresa was so deeply saddened by the plight of India's poor she left the comfort of Europe for the slums of Calcutta. Martin Luther King was grieved by the disparity between the ideals of America and the reality of life for minorities. It's the mother whose recent abortion has so compelled her to action that she ministers to other mothers in a similar plight.

Joyful are those who are deeply saddened to the point of action, for they will be comforted.

This isn't just true in theology. It's true in biology. Our bodies are telling us that it's OK, no, it is in fact essential to pay attention to the world as it is and the deep sorrow raging within as we acknowledge the fundamental brokenness.

Scientists can detect a substantive difference between tears that come from common experience (onions) and the tears of raw emotion. Literally, tears are cleansing to the soul.[3] What soap does for the body, tears do for the soul. Psalm 56:8 reminds us that God desires to record every tear we shed. For when we are so sad that we are moved to tears, the very action of crying is comforting. So Paul writes in 2 Corinthians 2:4: "For I wrote you out of great distress and anguish of heart and with many tears, not to grieve you but to let you know the depth of my love for you." Paul's tears were from the deep places of mourning in his own heart.

The writer of Revelation declares not that tears won't exist in the New Age but that all of our tears will be wiped by God's hand.

> "See, the home of God is among mortals,
> He will dwell with them as their God;
> they will be his peoples,
> and God himself will be with them;
> he will wipe every tear from their eyes.
> Death will be no more;
> mourning and crying and pain will be no more. . . .
> See, I am making all thing new."
> —Revelation 21:3–5a NRSV

The Gospel writers join the chorus of lament and hope in John 16:20: ". . . You will weep and mourn, but the world will rejoice; you will have pain, but your pain will turn into joy" (NRSV).

During Holy Week each year, Christians read from Luke 19 and soak in the image of Jesus overlooking the entire city of Jerusalem as he is on his way to the cross. Only Luke mentions the fact that Jesus weeps for the entire city. In context of Luke 19, Jesus weeps for two reasons. First, he understands the death, pain, disease, corruption, and sin that plague Jerusalem (as it does Rome). Second, he understands that this city too will one day be restored. He mourns in tears for the world as it is and the world as it will one day become. This isn't Jesus simply crying. This is mourning. And his mourning becomes action because his shed tears will, in just a few days, evolve into shed blood.

Heaven on earth. The Good Life breaking in now. Even as we wait.

One morning, the Episcopal priest and college professor Barbara Brown Taylor attempted to teach retreat participants about the necessity of understanding the profound connection between that which is spiritual and that which is physical and how the two cannot be separated. While exploring the Beatitudes, Taylor broke her students into groups of five and had them form a living *tableau*—which is a fancy French way of saying, a living demonstration, or living parable:

> As you can imagine, the resistance to doing this was enormous, verging on panic in a couple of cases. We were adults after all. Kids act things out. Adults discuss them.
>
> . . . The "Blessed Are Those Who Mourn" group came out—all women again—and arranged themselves around the woman who had volunteered to lie dead on the ground. A second woman sat down and cradled the first woman's head in her lap. Two others knelt beside her

31

and two others stood over them until they made a sort of cathedral over the dead woman's body. Everyone was touching someone so that they were all linked together, but . . . no one moved.

Those of us watching did not know what to do . . . Then, when the whole room was as still as a grave, the body of the woman on the floor began to heave. As her soft sobbing grew louder, the other women bent over it. Then one of them began to weep, and another gave a small, strangled yelp until the whole tableau was heaving ever so gently over the body of the dead woman who had come back to life.[4]

Several years ago, my wife's close friend, Mary, found out she had stage 4 colon cancer. All cancer is serious, but this was different. The cancer had been in her body for some time. She battled and fought against the cancer. She was overwhelmed. A few nights before she passed from this world to the next, she slipped into a comatose state. Early on the morning of her death, she awoke, sat straight up in bed, and offered a doxology. She sang her favorite songs,then she lay down, reentered her coma, and died. She left us as we knew her. She left us with a song dripping with the purification that only comes from suffering. *Praise went with her to the darkest moment. Doxology was with her when everyone else least expected it; when she needed it the most.* And indeed, we needed it, too. Later, in our mourning, her doxology companioned us. Mary's dying words comforted us; there in the very hours of her death, she was an agent of God's peace to us mourners.

What is true for us individually is also true for us collectively. God does for one what God longs to do for everyone.

How do we respond to the pain and suffering that haunts us? Something's amiss. Is life beautiful? Yes. But just on the horizon of its inherent beauty is a wild storm, waiting to tear everything to pieces, total destruction. Life is beautiful. But life is also deadly, depressing, and full of pain.

With so much pain, so much awareness of how *unheaven* earth really is, we need embodied answers to the question "How then shall we live?" Egypt, unlike many countries in the Middle East, has a "historic population of Christians, some 10 percent of the population, who trace their origins back to the apostle Mark."[5] Moreover, scholars believe that the man who carried Jesus' cross in Mark's Gospel, Simon of Cyrene, was an African.

Christians have suffered and mourned for decades.

On the outer edges of Cairo is a place called Mokkattam. Mokkattum is a sprawling slum near a large garbage dump. The slum, as you can imagine, smells putrid. Out of this unusual place, a vibrant Christian community has emerged. Instead of waging war against their enemies and foes, they are practicing the Jesus Promise that God can use tears to transform societies.

> Led by a priest in the Coptic Orthodox church, the community built houses, schools, a sports field, and a clinic at the foot of a mountain in an abandoned quarry. Around thirty years ago one of the slum dwellers stumbled across a large cave, and over time Coptic Christians moved one hundred

forty thousand tons of rock out of the cave to form a three-thousand seat auditorium. They worked mostly at night during Muslim fast periods, when the guards who might harass them went home to eat.[6]

Every week, Christian churches in America—black, white, Latino, Asian, as well as Methodist, Baptist, Community, Catholic, Episcopal, Churches of Christ—come together and sing praises to God. But most weeks, when we sing praises, we sing them individually from different places. We sing them from the place of a new job, unexpected pregnancy, or confirmation of God's presence. But we also sing praises from our dark places—the mother who buried her son when he was five, the father of the three whose wife left without the decency of a note, the unexpected divorce in the pillar family—we have to sing from those places too. Because both the peaks and the valleys are what make us human.

The real question is this: Why are we afraid to be the human God made us to be?

This demonstration plot of the Jesus Way has grown considerably. Currently the church in Mokkattam meets in a facility described as a 13,000-seat amphitheatre, also carved out of rock. It is, without any question, the largest Christian community in the entire Middle East.

Out of a garbage pit, *life.* Out of death*, resurrection.* Through tears*, healing.* Out of the earth, *heaven*. Out of the bad, *good*. Out of pain, *hope*. From mourning to dancing.

From despair to hope. From mourning to comfort.

Imagine the worship experience of 13,000 Egyptian Christians who've known suffering, isolation, marginalization, and oppression. They don't sing because they've avoided suffering and pain. They sing as we sing, because we experienced it, had it named, and still believe that God is moving in the world, preparing us for the great mystery of God's new heaven and new earth. When all will be well in the kingdom of God, tears will flow but God will wipe them all away.

When all of humanity experiences the final blessing Jesus promised so long ago, the world will be well because the world will be as it was meant to be.

So grieve deeply and grieve boldly. Suffer well. When you do it means you understand how broken the world is and how beautiful it might one day become. Mourning is the acute awareness that although God made the world the world is no longer the same world God originally made. Disappointment, hardship, pain, suffering, and absence are part of the ache reminding us that a different day, a new future is being foreshadowed in the life of Jesus. "Grieve, mourn and wail. Change your laughter to mourning and your joy to gloom. Humble yourselves before the Lord, and he will lift you up," writes Jesus' brother, James (4:9–10).

The elderly gentlemen leans in, whispering a profound truth to the young minister across the table. "You want to know about heaven in Judaism? Here it is. For the last several years I've cared for my wife. Day and night. Night and day. She suffered from Alzheimer's, memory loss, and paranoia. But one day, she remembered everything. Every detail of our marriage, names of children, places we'd visited. She wanted to dance, so we danced. The next day she died."

"I'm so sorry," said the young minister.

"I'm not. Right before she died, she looked at me and said, 'Can you see it? Can you see the beautiful city?'"—a reference to the notion of the heavenly city from heaven coming to earth.

"I thought I was giving my wife back to God. I was wrong. God was allowing me to peek into the future. God was giving my wife back to himself. And I got a glimpse of her returning back to the God who makes all things new."

Earth hasn't become heaven yet. That's why we mourn.

But it will. One day it will. And that's why Jesus said what he said.

We grieve and mourn but not as those who do so without hope, because God weeps with us now so God can laugh with us then.

CHAPTER 4

"Blessed are the meek,
for they will inherit the earth."
(Matthew 5:5)

GET SMALL

BIG AND SMALL

Heaven on earth comes to us in small doses, tiny hints, and small fragments.

Jesus teaches his disciples—then and now—the meaning of discipleship:

God's heart beats for the poor, the broken, the desperate; and the kingdom belongs to them.

God's promise to the broken is a future day of restoration.

Then, in his third statement of blessing, Jesus presents one of his most straightforward messages in all the Beatitudes—blessed are the meek, for they will inherit the earth. One scholar, Glen Stassen,

37

translates this verse: "Joyful are those whose wills are surrendered to God, for they will inherit the earth."[1] The word for meek (*praus*, pronounced pray-us) is often translated gentle or humble. But this doesn't quite capture the deeper meaning of the word. *Totally surrendered to God* means we understand who we are in proximity to God. That is, one understands one's inherent smallness in light of God's inherent largeness.

It means we revolve around God's life, not the other way around. Do you know the difference between me and God? God doesn't wake up in the morning thinking he's me. In the beginning, God made us in God's image. We've been returning the favor ever since.

To be small is not to suggest that one is insignificant. To be small simply means we properly understand who we are in light of God's big purpose, the kingdom.

In Matthew 11:28, Jesus invites his disciples to try his way of being small when he says regarding his strategy of smallness—"I am gentle and humble in heart, and you will find rest for your souls. For my yoke is easy and my burden is light" (in reference to the Beatitudes and Sermon on the Mount, no doubt).

Jesus demonstrates this fully later in the Gospel narrative by riding to Jerusalem, not on a powerful horse, but on a donkey. Every chance Jesus got, he got small.

Jesus was small before God. He got small. He chose to be small. He chose to see himself in right proximity to God. Because a new economy was being launched. The economy of heaven taking down the economy of earth. And when you are "meek" you are totally surrendered to God and you are smaller than you've ever been.

In this new way, a needed value emerged: *small was the new big*.

However, in American society in general and in local communities specifically we value popularity, attention, and celebrity. We like everything but "small"—we want it big, we want to be big, and we want it now.

Consider American fixation with celebrity culture as an example of our love of size.

> Why do we crave celebrities? Here's my theory: To be human is to feel inconsequential. So we worship celebrities and we seek to look like them. All the great things they have done we identify with in order to escape our own inconsequential lives. But it's so dumb. With this stream of perfectly airbrushed, implanted, liposuctioned stars, you would have to be an absolute powerhouse of self-esteem already not to feel totally inferior before them. So we worship them because we feel inconsequential, but doing it makes us feel even worse. We make them stars, but then their fame makes us feel insignificant. I am part of this whole process as an editor. No wonder I feel soiled at the end of the day.[2]

But not so with Jesus' new way of being human. Not so with the kingdom, for in this project those who get close to God are those who choose to get small by total surrender.

This isn't a concept Jesus invents. It is, however, a concept he perfects. Jesus was so moved by the stories of Torah that he sought to live Torah as a Hollywood actor lives out a script. The teachings of Torah became so much a part of Jesus' imagination, he simply improvised and enacted ancient stories in fresh ways. If Martin Luther King, Jr. is right—that every expression of love grows out of a consistent total surrender to God—our place in God's bigness is worth exploring.

Stories of small overcoming big are the kinds of stories that shaped Jesus' spirituality and God-view. Small is the new big.

Israel overcomes Egypt.

David defeats Goliath.

Gideon, despite a lackluster army, goes on the offensive.

Naaman, the mighty warrior, is changed by a child.

Zacchaeus catches the attention and affection of Jesus.

These stories embody exactly what Jesus says in the Sermon on the Mount. *Blessed are the meek, for they will inherit the earth.*

CREATION SMALLNESS

God's choice to work through smallness is even evident in nature. Psalm 33:6–9 makes this claim:

> By the word of the Lord the heavens were made,
>> their starry host by the breath of his mouth.
> He gathers the waters of the sea into jars;
>> he puts the deep into storehouses.
> Let all the earth fear the Lord;
>> let all the people of the world revere him.
> For he spoke, and it came to be;
>> he commanded, and it stood firm.

And yet here we are, "fearfully and wonderfully made" (Psalm 139:14), made up of one cell from our father and one cell from our mother. Twenty-eight chromosomes come together to give us the beauty that is one human being. God takes the smallest elements of physical creation and does something big.

A friend recently showed me a ground-breaking picture captured by NASA. The picture is taken from an epic 3.7 billion miles away from earth. The picture was captured by a NASA exploratory satellite some thirteen years after launch. The satellite went further. There were a million more galaxies, billions of more miles away, but any further out and we could no longer see that little dot in the lower right-hand side of the picture. That little dot is the planet Earth. Carl Sagan noted the importance of our smallness:

> From this distant vantage point, the Earth might not seem of particular interest. But for us, it's different. Consider again that dot. That's here, that's home, that's us. On it everyone you love, everyone you know, everyone you ever heard of, every human being who ever was, lived out their lives. The aggregate of our joy and suffering, thousands of confident religions, ideologies, and economic doctrines, every hunter and forager, every hero and coward, every creator and destroyer of civilization, every king and peasant, every young couple in love, every mother and father, hopeful child, inventor and explorer, every teacher of morals, every corrupt politician, every "superstar," every "supreme leader," every saint and sinner in the history of our species lived there—on a mote of dust suspended in a sunbeam.[3]

I had an experience in creation a few years ago that forced me to deal with my smallness. The bigger I am the smaller God is. The smaller I become, the bigger God becomes. This is creation's chief gift to humanity—we are reminded of who we really are and who we are not.

Several years ago, while pursuing a graduate degree in theology, I served as an assistant basketball coach at a university in Texas. The first week on the job, the head coach (my boss) walked into my office with the other assistant coach and declared, "Boys, we're going on a road trip. We need to spend some time with each other out of the office." As he said this, he placed on an 8x10 photo of Pike's Peak on my desk, one of the largest open-trail mountain summits in the United States "We're going to climb Pike's Peak in one day."

Sure we are, I thought to myself.

My heart went into my stomach. Though I'd played college basketball, I had spent all my time the previous year in the library studying theology—I was in no shape to do this. Neither were my two friends.

We drove from West Texas to the Colorado Springs area the night before we were to climb. I informed my friends that I needed to go to Wal-Mart. "Why?" they inquired.

"Because I need some supplies."

"You mean you didn't bring anything with you?"

"I brought my shorts, running shoes, and a few granola bars."

"Are you serious?"

"Yes, I'm serious." A long pause ensued. Maybe I'd lose my job.

We overslept the next morning. This is a crucial detail to include because the window for summiting Pike's Peak is small during August. That is, you can get caught in a lightning storm or blizzard if you don't reach the summit before early afternoon.

The first stretch of the hike was fine save the fact that I thought my heart was going to burst. Apparently this whole "acclamation" thing that real hikers talk about is serious business. We got to the halfway point in decent shape. I should note that it's called the halfway point but it's really like the one quarter point because the next stretch of terrain is much more difficult than the beginning part. I recall seeing two Scandinavian hiker-types staring me down. Their eyes said, "I can bench press you, city slicker."

About an hour into this second portion of the hike, the temperature began to drop and I'm thinking that my shorts, tank-top, and three-dollar pullover might not get the job done. All of a sudden, lightning began ripping through the sky. Here, in this moment of fright, I gained one of my first lessons in hiking.

When a 6'4" human being is walking beyond the tree line, said person becomes the tree. We were totally exposed and in a dangerous place. Being big isn't all it's cracked up to be.

One of us in the group, I can't remember who, became convinced (probably due to a lack of oxygen) that our cell phones were conductors and that we needed to throw them down the side of the mountain. Slightly less dumb heads prevailed and we continued to walk. About thirty minutes into the lightning storm, a blizzard broke out. I've seen my share of snow (I grew up in a city surrounded by lakes—we invented lake-effect snow) but nothing like this. It came out of nowhere. I could barely see five feet ahead of me. After another thirty minutes or so of walking in this blizzard with the lightning, we found a cave. It was like finding a pool of water in the middle of a dry desert. We huddled inside the cave (one member of our group tried calling his wife in case he didn't "make it") only to find there were some other hikers already inside the cave. These hikers, who looked professional compared to the look-what-the-cat-drug-in crew before their eyes, were warming themselves with special blankets (I came to find out later they were space blankets). "What on God's green earth are you doing here?" one man asked.

I thought I'd be helpful and replied, "We're trying to make it to the summit." I can't repeat what he said to me. The FCC would come after me.

Here's the gist of his speech: You don't belong up here. You have not prepared. You don't have a guide (Pike's Peak at the time was the highest climb available to people without guides); you don't know where you are going or what you are doing. People die every week on this mountain because they think they can do this alone, but they can't.

I was puffed up, a former college athlete who was still a legend in my own mind. I was big. It took a mountain to remind me how small I am.

Small is the new big.

Because what is true in Scripture is true in creation. And what is true in Scripture and creation is always true in Jesus. Small is the new big. Small doesn't mean insignificant.

Paul says Jesus "humbled himself" (Philippians 2), which is to say, once Jesus became small, God did something big. Jesus got small, God made him big.

This is the heart of Jesus' kingdom movement. This is what God is doing.

Jesus chooses two interesting words in Matthew 5:5: *praus* (pray-us) and *ge* (gay); again, meek and earth. *Meek* means to be completely surrendered to the will of God. The word comes from an agrarian context: the harnessed strength of a horse. The word is also written in plural. It's about a community of people surrendered to God not simply isolated individuals. *Earth* is a reference to the eschatological hope of the Jews that the Messiah would not only redeem a people but that the Messiah might also redeem the land of God's chosen.

Only the small, the surrendered-to-God-in-all-things, will really be at the center of what God is doing in the next chapter. "You who wish to possess the earth now, take care. If you are meek, you will posses it; if ruthless, the earth will possess you," whispers Augustine many centuries later.[4] Blessed are the meek for one day they might actually desire possession of the land.

To be meek is not to simply be modest or humble. To be meek is to know exactly who you are (a human created in God's image) and exactly who you aren't (God). Experience, Scripture, creation, and instinct should be constant reminders of this truth. To be meek is to be small. Small in all things. It doesn't mean false humility or low self-esteem. It means deferential to God and all the people God has placed around you.

It's about proximity, seeing yourself as small in the grand scheme of God. But not so small you deem your life insignificant.

Abba Macarius, a fourth-century monk in Egypt, met up with the devil one day while walking down the road. The devil repeatedly attacked the monk to no avail. "What is your power, Macarius, that makes me powerless against you? All that you do, I do too. You fast, but I never eat. You keep vigil, but I never sleep. In one thing only do you beat me." The monk wanted to know the secret of his apparent success. The devil responded, "Your humility. Because of that I can do nothing against you."[5]

From Celsius to Nietzsche, from Caesar to Hitler—many have charged Christianity with being a religion of weakness. And on this point, and this point only, they are right.

A bunch of weak disciples, following a weak Messiah have changed the course of human history like no other movement.

Blessed are the meek. The earth belongs to them.

Because . . .

Small is God's *big*.

I had an e-mail exchange with an aspiring actor from NYC about being a "big" actor versus being a "small" actor, a B actor, or even an *extra*. He wrote these insightful words that I think sum up exactly what Jesus was describing in his beatitude on meekness. Todd told me he preferred taking the small roles:

The extras are the backbone in production. Our job is to fill the scene, create ambiance, and provide a struggle for the Principals (main actors) and so on. We provide a world full of interest that, without us, would be extremely bland and we know this and . . . we use it to our advantage when necessary. The payoff is mostly very little. You stand out in the cold all day in the street while arching your head way up at the top of a building where, supposedly, Sam Worthington is going to jump off (*Man On a Ledge*). You get a boxed lunch; you wait in line for 2 hours to get your papers signed, and then see you only made $150 that day. Not worth it, no payoff. Then another day you're with Will Smith or Steve Buscemi and eating a feast and making good money. I think, deep down, what makes me do it is the continual appreciation for my craft and everything that goes into it. I've worked so hard to get to where I am and I had no clue what the other side of the industry is. So, for me, I figured I would venture out on my own ledge and try it. Whether it's Movies or TV or Theatre, people depend on these things to get them through hard times or to pick them up and it's this give and take of acting that makes it work. Knowing that I may or may not be seen doesn't stop me because I know I am part of the bigger picture. Whatever the experience, I know I am at least working and trying to make something of my life. It's been incredibly eye opening which is the greatest payoff. Story telling is such an ancient art and it's important that we continue to do so. All artists are story tellers and a story cannot be told simply by its main characters. You have to have the best friend, or the crazy co worker, or the dreaded in laws to really grasp the whole picture. One of my favorite painters is Georges Seurat and he's most famous for his painting *A Sunday Afternoon on the Island of La Grande Jatte*. He was a pointillist painter and his huge piece of art depicting this park full of people is made up simply of tiny dots. The painting as a whole is really beautiful, but to move in closer and look at the intricate display of colored dots [that] create the actual picture is nearly breathtaking. *I love and live . . . to be that dot.*

CRAVING GOD'S FUTURE

*"Blessed are those who hunger and
thirst for righteousness,
for they will be filled."
(Matthew 5:6)*

TWO FACES OF AMERICA: MALCOLM AND MARTIN

I became obsessed with Malcolm X after my eleventh-grade teacher challenged me, a relatively aimless high school student, to read his autobiography. I shrugged off the assignment for two weeks, but one night, when nothing was on TV [or whatever], I picked up The *Autobiography of Malcolm X* and was hooked. True to Malcolm's often abrasive persona ("We didn't land on Plymouth Rock, Plymouth Rock landed on *us*"), this landmark book chronicles Malcolm's thoughts on American politics, racism, drugs, incarceration, and family tragedy. It also brought attention to the paradoxical state of American Christianity: a religion built on the premise of inclusion and reconciliation was in fact propagating hate, division, and oppression on the shores of America.

Malcolm's description of the hypocrisy of Christianity and its place in American society is bold and sometimes hard for Christians to read.[1] He describes a scene from his Nebraska childhood in which a group of Ku Klux Klansmen rode to his home. Displaying their weapons, the men demanded that Malcolm's father come out. Because Malcolm's father was away on church business, his mother, Mrs. Little, came to the door, allowing the Klansmen to see her pregnant condition. The men threatened her family and said that they'd better get out of town because the "good Christian white people" were not going to stand for Mr. Little's spreading trouble among the good Negroes. Malcolm relayed his mother's vivid recollection of that night: "Still shouting threats, the Klansmen finally spurred their horses and galloped around the house, shattering every window pane with their gun butts. Then they rode off into the night, their torches flaring, as suddenly as they had come."

Physical violence haunted their family in the form of the Black Legion—a Michigan version of the Ku Klux Klan.

Malcolm writes about the day when he returned home with three siblings and noticed that his mother and father were engaging in a heated conversation. Evidently, there had been quite a bit of tension because of threats posed by the Black Legion. Mr. Little became angry, and he walked out the door to calm his nerves.

Malcolm's dad did not return. Malcolm recalls his mother's continuing anxiety that evening as she clutched the children at bedtime. Malcolm remembers waking to the sound of his mother's screaming voice. The police were in his living room.

> My mother was taken by the police to the hospital, and to a room where a sheet was over my father in a bed, and she wouldn't look, she was afraid to look. Probably it was wise that she didn't. My father's skull, on one side, was crushed in, I was told later. Negroes in Lansing have always whispered that he was attacked and then laid across some tracks for a streetcar to run over him. His body was cut almost in half.

The children awoke the next morning to learn what had taken place in Christian America: a group of religious men had taken the life of a black preacher in the name of God. "It was morning when we children at home got the word that he was dead. I was six. I can remember a vague commotion, the house filled up with people crying, saying bitterly that the white Black Legion had finally gotten him. My mother was hysterical. In the bedroom, women were holding smelling salts under her nose. . . ."

When the Little's insurance company refused to pay the family the money they rightfully deserved, the family could no longer function. The state moved in, disbanded the Little family, pushing Malcolm's mother to a nervous breakdown. Eventually, Mrs. Little "went crazy" and spent the majority of her adult life in a psychiatric home outside of Lansing. Malcolm would never recover from such brutality.

Some biographers claim that Malcolm's five brothers were killed by white men.

After several emotional breakdowns, Mrs. Little hit rock bottom. When she sent to live in a state-run mental ward, the children were split up, each sent to various foster homes to live with white families. Life spun out of control and in just a few short years, Malcolm Little, now known as the Civil Rights voice, Malcolm X, found himself in prison. The son of a Baptist preacher, who endured the murder of his father, went to prison and became a Muslim powerhouse. I've often wondered what Malcolm might have become had he been introduced, in life experience, to the gospel of Jesus in the Sermon on the Mount and not the gospel of American privilege and exclusion.[2]

"Tenderness is love felt in private. Justice is love experienced in public," writes Cornel West.[3] Malcolm was hungry for private tenderness and public justice. Hungry for love.

Martin Luther King, Jr. was another Baptist preacher's son (and most white Americans are more familiar with King than with Malcolm and Earl Little). King grew up in Atlanta, raised under the care, discipline, and passion of his father, Daddy King. A self-made preacher, Daddy King taught himself to read as a teenager. From early on, Martin Luther (whose birth name Michael was changed by his father to Martin because his father intuitively knew his boy was going to be a great preacher) displayed a remarkable gift for oratory. Although Martin failed to excel early on, friends knew that God had done something special with this aspiring young leader.

Daddy King pushed Martin to reach his potential. After graduating early from Morehouse College in Atlanta, King moved to Pennsylvania where he attended Crozer Seminary and became enthralled with the role of Christianity in human history to accomplish great things for God (as well as the often hypocritical state of Christian leaders regarding matters of race and economics). Following seminary, Martin, determined to become a leading academic, attended Boston University in the early 1950s. King flourished at Boston University where his handle on the biblical text and contemporary experience set him apart. He was a genius with the spoken word, painting the imagination with God's grace the way Michelangelo used a paintbrush.

Most of Martin's friends believed he would graduate and join the academy. But something would not allow Martin to leave the call to preach. Call it God (or his Daddy's stern admonition) King, at the young age of twenty-six, became the pastor of Dexter Avenue Baptist church in Montgomery, Alabama. Just two years later, King became the face of black resistance to Jim Crow segregation. Not bad for someone who'd not yet turned thirty. King's struggle to hear God's call to engage the issues of injustice is often glossed over.

King's legacy is perhaps the most chronicled legacy in twentieth-century American history.[4] Through prophetic speech, creative resistance, and unwavering loyalty to the nonviolence of Jesus in the Sermon on the Mount, King forever altered the trajectory of oppressed groups around the world in their quest for democracy.

These two uniquely American stories of justice remind Christians that one of our primary tasks as disciples is to help God bring about the justice and righteousness that God yearns for. We have an obligation to help transform a world marred by oppression into the world Isaiah spoke about, the world Micah spoke about: a world characterized by God's justice. Malcolm and Martin, in their own way, are mirrors showing us our own struggle to become the people God intended us to be. Injustice generally and racism specifically continue to afflict our society. American soil—from the early days of our history, through the Civil War, to the Civil Rights Movement on the red clay of the South—cries out for more:

More justice.

More truth-telling.

More repentance.

More gospel.

More heaven-on-earth.

More God.

More Jesus.

More of the Good Life.

CRAVING GOD'S FUTURE

We become interested in justice when it concerns us. Malcolm X's story, in America, is interesting to white readers but it does not typically evoke—as it does in the black community—outrage, public anger, and wounds. Why? Because, as human beings, we are usually interested in justice when it concerns me/us not someone else, someone outside our immediate community.

What does the Muslim leader from the northeast and a Baptist preacher from Atlanta have to do with the Sermon on the Mount? At an elementary level, they remind us what we know from our childhood playground experiences: no one likes to be wronged. Martin and Malcolm, admittedly larger-than-life figures, remind us of this on a large-scale basis. If it's true for a few it might just be true for most.

When I was a teacher at a liberal arts college in suburban Detroit, I often taught a freshman seminar called "Jesus and Justice." I asked students to share stories about a time when they felt they'd been treated unfairly. One student got so into the telling of her personal injustice story, in which relatives had stolen money from her when her parents died in a tragic car accident, her face got red, her hands shook, and her voice cracked as she retold her experience, a story of injustice perpetrated by those who were called to love her.

Amidst injustice and outrage, Jesus' message is birthed into the world through the Sermon on the Mount. Traditional translations read like this: *Blessed are those who hunger and thirst for righteousness, for they will be filled.* What if you heard it a slightly different way? *Blessed are those who crave justice, for only God will satisfy them.* If the word *justice* seems too strong a translation for righteousness it's because of the parody we've made of the word *righteousness*. In Greek, the same word used to describe righteousness is also used to describe justice.

The word *righteousness* conjures meanings around personal piety, religious devotion, or consistent discipline. In other circles, the word is about what God has done for the individual. Righteousness is not so much about virtue ("Are you righteous?") as it is God's purposes for the world. In the Hebrew Scriptures, a consistent theme emerges concerning God's thirst for justice. Righteousness in the Old Testament means "restorative justice." That is, righteousness and justice are aimed at the broken pieces of a community's life being put back together.

Righteousness and justice are about families, societies—the entire world—put back together, made whole.

In that sense, righteousness and justice take on a robust identity: poverty, homelessness, AIDS, orphan care are righteousness and justice issues. Other righteousness and justice issues include caring for the elderly, support for single moms, suicide prevention, and addiction counseling. For every way society is broken, drowning in the power of sin's force, that's how many people God raises up to participate in the Restoration Project. In that sense, every ministry is a righteousness and justice ministry because both are ultimately about restoration.

Righteousness is about one's personal role (prompted by grace and power) in the repairing of God's world. The personal and the public cannot be separated if our ethic is based upon the life of Jesus. Consider these Isaiah texts that exemplify the robust meanings of the Hebrew and Greek words for righteousness and justice remembering that Isaiah was the Bible Jesus quotes or alludes to more than any other Hebrew work.[5] In the Hebrew language the words used for "straight," "righteousness," and "justice" are always in relationship to each other. To walk along "straight paths" is to walk in the "paths of righteousness."[6] Eighteen times the prophet Isaiah parallels righteousness *with* justice (for example, 1:27; 9:7; 33:15; 56:1; 59:14); they are intricately related. These two words were never intended to be separated. Doing the right thing—whether individually (righteousness) or collectively (justice)—is always a primary interest of God in the prophets, because a life is the totality of choices made for the individual and the community.

One of the most important examples of the twin-pairing of righteousness and justice comes from Isaiah 9: For a child has been born to us, a son given to us; authority rests upon his shoulders; and he is named Wonderful Counselor, Mighty God, Everlasting Father, Prince of Peace. His authority shall grow continually and there shall be peace for the throne of David and his kingdom (see Isaiah 9:6–7).

The Bible Jesus read contained the words of the prophet Isaiah. Jesus probably read the prophetic book often. For the Old Testament prophets, particularly Isaiah, righteousness was synonymous with justice. For Isaiah *justice* referred to not just to the wrongdoer being punished, it could also refer to any kind of wrong situation being made *right* or straight.

In the Law of the Old Testament when someone who stole something from somebody else was punished that person also had to pay back what they stole plus a fifth of its value on top of that (Exodus 22).

This is called "restitution." Restitution is considered part of justice as well.

Justice isn't just about the punishment of the wrongdoer; it's about making provision for what the one done wrong had lost. This is one example of someone stealing from another. The point is attempting to right the wrong—replacing what's been lost or taken—is considered part of justice, too.

Throughout the Old Testament—the hungry being fed, the sick being made well, those in need being cared for—were all situations considered by the prophets to be expressions of justice, of making things right, of straightening things out.

So "justice" didn't always have to do with punishing a wrongdoer but also helping to right a situation in someone's life.

Biblically speaking, justice or righteousness can be related to caring for the elderly, helping someone find freedom from addiction, attempting to save a marriage, helping a family experience reconciliation.

In other words, when Jesus called for justice and righteousness, he was calling for any and all action that attempted to make things right in the world.

The Gospels are filled with reminders that God yearns for righteousness—and that God expects human beings to help set oppressive situations to rights. Perhaps the parable that best embodies Jesus' understanding of righteousness and justice is the parable of the workers in the vineyard, in Matthew 20. A group of workers is hired at six in the morning, followed by other groups at nine, noon, three, and five. The late workers, the guys who a) wanted to work but couldn't find any or

b) slept in because they'd partied the night before, stood around most of the day. Yet, the latecomers get paid the same amount as the guys who had to scrape the ice off their car windows before the sun came up. *"It's not fair!"* Jesus was thinking of what a worker needs to feed his family. He was thinking of the kind of justice that delivers unemployed workers from their need. Twice in the parable, the owner says he is doing what is just (verses 4 and 13), which is a stark reminder about the nature of the kingdom (verse 1)—the kingdom is an extension of God's justice. And this particular kind of justice is in the midst of human community. This is why, for instance, just one chapter later, Jesus chastises Jewish leaders for not understanding the fullness and depth of being righteous. He says to them, "the tax collectors and prostitutes of our day understand God's Big Dream for the world better than you because you are focused on self and not the world!" (21:32, author's paraphrase).

Righteousness is about hungering and thirsting for things to be made right. Trying to be pious without engaging God in the world or trying to engage the world without the disciplines of study, fasting, and prayer—either way, you are trying to dance with one leg. Ever try it? Difficult. Ever try to do it well? Impossible.[7] Paul, no doubt influenced by the tenor of Isaiah, wrote to a struggling church in Corinth: "God made [Jesus] who had no sin to be sin for us, so that we might become the *righteousness* of God" (2 Corinthians 5:21, emphasis added).

THE VOICE

In his provocative book, *Simply Christian*, N. T. Wright makes the persuasive claim that our human longing for justice reminds us that human beings are created in God's image. Wright uses the metaphor of voice and echoes. He argues that there is one voice, one Speaker. Our hunger for justice, beauty, truth, relationships is merely an echo of the voice. There are three ways, Wright says, that we can explain the echo of justice. First, we can dismiss it as mere fantasy. Or, we can talk about a world that has nothing to do with this world, we can only dream about it—there will be righteousness in heaven, later on. Perhaps there's a third option: The voice we hear speaking into our ear that there is more to this world than this world knows is a gift from God. It's an echo that points us back to the One speaking. " . . . There is someone speaking to us, whispering in our inner ear—someone who cares very much about this present world and our present selves, and who has made us and the world for a purpose which will indeed involve justice . . . the world being rescued at last."[8]

The reason we have a passion for equality and justice is because we have heard, deep within ourselves, "the echo of a voice which calls us to live like that." That is, we pursue righteousness and justice because we are from God and we are called to co-create with God, partnering to bring about God's passions in the world through our work, art, storytelling, protest, speech, and action.

Jews call this *tikkun olam*—people's participation, with God, in restoring creation, in putting back together the pieces of a broken creation. The call to *tikkun olam* is the call to partner with God in restoring all things.

When righteousness and justice come together, *tikkun olam* is birthed.

Righteousness and justice necessarily work in tandem. Both elements are required. Like dancing with both legs. You can dance on one leg but you won't do it well nor for very long. Both legs are required.

My friend Kevin is a water engineer. He's trying to figure out how to bring clean water to nine thousand Mayans in the Ulpan Valley, Guatemala. Eighty-year-old women and young children walk two hours each way for fresh water and Kevin is dreaming up ways to bring it to them within a ten-minute stroll.

My father works at Children's Hospital in downtown Detroit. He runs an E.C.M.O. (Extracorporeal Membrane Oxygenation) unit and works as a respiratory therapist with children who cannot breathe on their own. He often works with the babies born with drug and alcohol addiction—addictions passed on from their mothers.

Tikkun olam. It's a beautiful tradition that anyone can participate in. It's a song we can all dance to.

When I was a freshman in college (1997), my mother gave me a New Revised Standard Version (NRSV) of the Bible. On the inside cover she wrote these words, "Stay hungry and thirsty for God's word . . . and you will always be filled!"—an obvious reference to Matthew

5:6. When I read that inscription, I immediately thought my mom was challenging me to a private ethical life (of course, that's not true but it's what I thought). As I came to really study and know the Jesus my mother and father spent their lives pointing me toward, the meaning of Matthew 5:6 grew, expanded, totally consuming me. Now I know what Jesus was saying and doing. Hungering and thirsting for righteousness was a way of getting me to see the brokenness of the world and the possibilities of God. Every inch of creation is drenched in the divine presence.

When a vision for God's future infuses its way into your imagination—what Jesus called your heart, soul, strength, and mind—it's only then that your belly will be full of gospel food. Blessed are those who crave God's future. That's food. Soul food. Food that never runs out. Water that is always available. The psalmist and Jesus are singing the same tune: "As the deer pants for streams of water, / so my soul pants for you, my God" (Psalm 42:1). Because when we crave God's future we are first and foremost craving God.

And that, at last, will be enough. Because God is enough.

CHAPTER 6

*"Blessed are the merficul,
for they will be shown mercy."
(Matthew 5:7)*

MERCY ME

There's an old story about a cattle rancher who was told that a young cowhand had been caught in the act of stealing one of his cows. When the thief was dragged before the rancher, he looked down at the frightened youth and said, "Hang him. Nothing personal, son. I like you a lot, you understand. But we have rules here in the West. Besides, it will teach you a lesson."

One day, the old rancher died and appeared before the judgment seat of God. As he stood there, he remembered all the mean, horrible things he had done over the course of his life. He stood there, trembling in his boots, when God looked down upon him, in mercy and tenderness, and said, "Forgive him. It will teach him a lesson."

God wants to teach us mercy, but he's not waiting until we appear before his judgment seat. He does it from a mount at the very beginning of Jesus' ministry. Jesus' proclamation concerning mercy follows on the heels of his proclamation concerning hungering and thirsting for things in our world to be made right. Without mercy, things can't be made right. Many of us have a tendency today to see justice and mercy as polar opposites of one another. In the ways of God, though, mercy is the means by which justice—God's justice—comes to pass. Through acts of mercy his kingdom is administered and his dreams for the world are realized.

It's probable that Jesus' proclamation concerning mercy raised some eyebrows. According to some Greco-Roman philosophical traditions of Jesus' day, mercy was not always seen as worthy of celebration or emulation.[1] It was contrary to the Roman idea of justice because it involved providing unearned help or relief. To show mercy was to show favor upon someone who had done nothing to deserve whatever was being given to them. Showing mercy was counterintuitive to the idea of how one secures and maintains power and control. If you show mercy you're going to wind up being taken advantage of and, in the end, lose influence, power, resources, or people's fear of you. Finally, showing mercy wasn't how the Roman gods ran things "up there" or "down here"—that's just not the way reality worked—you better look after yourself![2] Jesus makes clear that not only does God show mercy, but God is looking after the lives of those who are showing mercy. This is how God runs his kingdom. Those who are merciful are not nearly as at risk as people think they are—because God is watching after the merciful.

This would prove to be the first of many attempts by Jesus to reach the religious leaders of God's people who had lost touch with the importance of mercy. As surprising as this may be to some today, mercy was at the heart of much of the law of the Old Testament.[3] As we read through the Gospels, it becomes apparent that the religious leaders had lost sight of what the prophet Micah said about God, "And what does the Lord require of you? To act justly and to love mercy and to walk humbly with your God. . . . [God delights] to show mercy" (Micah 6:8; 7:18). God delights to show mercy! The theme of mercy is woven throughout the rest of the Sermon on the Mount when it comes to what Jesus has to say about those who do us wrong, how we should treat our enemies, and how we should respond to people in need. Jesus' instruction for how we handle every one of those situations is grounded in mercy.

Beyond the Sermon on the Mount, Jesus keeps mercy ever before the religious leaders, calling them back to it time and time again. In Matthew 9, the religious leaders react negatively to Jesus being seen eating with tax collectors and notorious "sinners" and Jesus responds, "Go and learn what this means: 'I desire *mercy*, not sacrifice.' For I have not come to call the righteous, but sinners" (Matthew 9:12–13, emphasis added). For Jesus, eating with sinners was an expression of mercy. In quoting from the prophet Hosea, Jesus was saying that God desired the show of mercy toward another human being more than the worship ritual of a sacrifice within the Temple. Jesus again quotes the very same verse to the religious leaders in Matthew 12 when he laments, "If you had known what these words mean, 'I desire *mercy*, not sacrifice . . .'" (Matthew 12:7, emphasis added). Jesus doesn't let up but continues to drive home mercy in Matthew 23, "Woe to you, teachers of the law and Pharisees, you hypocrites! You give a tenth of your spices. . . . But you have neglected the more important matters of the law—justice, *mercy* and faithfulness. You should have practiced the latter, without neglecting the former" (Matthew 23:23, emphasis added). Jesus chastises them for being so meticulous about giving a tithe at the Temple on everything they have, but not being attentive to the more important matters of the law involving mercy toward others. Many tend to think of "worshipping" God as strictly *vertical*—something that happens between an individual and God within "temple walls" and religious rituals. But God's value on mercy reminds us that "worshipping" God is every bit as *horizontal* as it is vertical—it involves a lifestyle of mercy toward others beyond "temple walls" and religious rituals. He calls us to *love* mercy (Micah 6:8) and *learn it* (Matthew 9:12).

THE LEARNING CURVE OF MERCY

The word *mercy* begins with *me*. Becoming merciful has a lot to do with having awakened to our own need for mercy. Studies have shown that those who live closer to the poverty line give a greater percentage of their income to charitable causes than those who don't live anywhere near the poverty line.[4] Could this be because those living closer to the poverty line have experience themselves with being acutely in need of mercy? The truth is all of us are below the poverty line when it comes to our lack of righteousness before God.

There could be something to the order of the way the Beatitudes unfold in this regard. Perhaps the only way to embrace the reality Jesus spoke of in Matthew 5:7 is through first acknowledging the reality spoken of in Matthew 5:3—that we're poor in spirit, spiritually bankrupt— that we don't have what it takes, in and of ourselves, to be made right and make the world right. We need the mercy of God.

In 2001, Tim Goeglein started running the White House Office of Public Liaison, which provided him daily access to then-President George W. Bush. All of that ended abruptly, though, in February of 2008 when it was discovered that twenty-seven out of thirty-nine published articles of Goeglein's were plagiarisms. When the facts came out, his career in the White House was over immediately.

Goeglein readily admitted he was guilty. It began a personal crisis unlike any he had ever known in his life, bringing great humiliation to his wife, children, closest friends, and to the president whom he had represented for eight years.

Goeglein was summoned to the White House after his dismissal to face the president. Once inside the Oval Office, Goeglein immediately said, "Mr. President, I owe you an . . ."

Bush simply said, "Tim, you are forgiven."

It took Goeglein by surprise, but he tried again to finish his apology, "But, sir . . ."

Bush interrupted him again, "Stop. I have known grace and mercy in my life, and you are forgiven."

After a long talk, a healing process was launched for Goeglein that he later credited as a spiritual turning point in his life.[5] Bush's experience with mercy in his own life had made a difference in how he responded to Goeglein.

"DESERVE" HAS NOTHING TO DO WITH IT

In John Fischer's *12 Steps for the Recovering Pharisee (Like Me)*, step 3 involves admitting that we detest mercy being given to those who, unlike us, haven't worked for it and don't deserve it. When one speaks of mercy as though it is something to be worked for or deserved, it's a pretty good clue the person has yet to understand mercy. Mercy's not a wage. It's a gift.

The story goes that a woman appeared before Napoleon to plead for her son's life as he was about to be executed. Napoleon responded that the punishment fit the crime. It was justice.

The woman responded, "I'm not here to talk about justice. I'm here to plead for mercy."

Napoleon said, "He doesn't deserve mercy."

She responded, "It wouldn't be mercy if he deserved it. Therefore, mercy is what I ask."

It's said that Napoleon was so taken by her response he granted her son a pardon.

"Deserve" has nothing to do with mercy. The psalmist puts it this way in Psalm 103:10, "He does not treat us as our sins deserve." That's what makes it mercy. We extend it not because of the character of others but because of the character of our King and how he has treated us.

MERCY IS AS MERCY DOES

Mercy is an action more than an attitude. Grammatically speaking, *mercy* may be the subject of the previous sentence, but in reality it's a verb. The word for *merciful* in Matthew 5:7 is *eleemones*. It can mean "generous in deeds of deliverance."

Mercy is often associated with forgiveness, and rightfully so when one considers the weighty teaching on mercy and forgiveness in places like Matthew 18. One of our greatest needs as human beings is to be delivered from a bondage to guilt in the wake of our sins against God and others (see Psalm 32:1–5). Mercy's expression is not limited to forgiveness, though. Mercy makes a difference for those with needs of various kinds—be they physical, mental, spiritual, or material. Later in the Sermon on the Mount, Jesus will speak of giving to the needy (Matthew 6:2). The word *give* is *eleemosyen*. Look again at the similarity of those two words—*eleemones* (merciful) and *eleemosyen* (give). The word for *give* is from the same root word as the word for *mercy*. *Giving mercy* could, in one sense, be considered redundant. Mercy is as mercy does.

As the rest of the Sermon on the Mount and the Gospel of Matthew unfold we see mercy in action in a variety of ways. It's at the heart of providing the poor with economic resources (5:42; 6:2–4; 25:31–46). It's embodied in extending love to our enemies and forgiveness to those who've sinned against us (5:38–43; 6:12, 14–15). Mercy is what Jesus referred to as the reason he was eating with tax collectors and sinners (9:13). It is mercy being called for by those seeking Jesus' deliverance from their (or their loved ones') struggle with disease and demonic oppression (9:27; 15:22; 17:15; 20:30–31). Mercy has many faces, but it is a common denominator in much of what happens when the kingdom of heaven breaks forth. Mercy is as mercy does.

Perhaps no story more succinctly and beautifully expresses mercy in action as the story of the good Samaritan (Luke 10:25–37). A man is hijacked by robbers while traveling along a road—beaten and left for dead in a ditch. A priest sees him and crosses over to the other side of the road and passes by him; so does a Levite—both of them recognized symbols of religious piety. But then, of all things, a Samaritan, a "low-life" in Jewish eyes, saw the man and took action to help him—binding his wounds, getting him a place to stay and heal, and paying for it all.

Jesus asks this question, " 'Which of these three do you think was a neighbor to the man who fell into the hands of robbers?' The expert in the law replied, 'The one who had mercy on him.' Jesus told him, 'Go and do likewise' " (Luke 10:36–37). Notice that Jesus didn't say, "Go and feel likewise." Mercy is as mercy does. Mercy is like faith—without works, it is dead.

When Bob Riley was elected governor of Alabama in 2002, he was known for being a conservative who had won the Friend of Taxpayers Award several years in a row. But when he became governor he found that the tax code had not changed since 1901 and that the richest in Alabama paid 3 percent of their income in taxes while the poorest paid up to 12 percent.

Alabama was 47th in the US in total taxes—its schools had been underfunded for years and ranked among the bottom in the country in effectiveness. So Riley proposed a tax hike among the middle and high-income households to help the schools out, as well as the poor. He went on to argue that it was their Christian duty to look after the poor more carefully.

His proposal was defeated. One political leader who had fought against Riley's proposal said, "You'll find most Alabamians have got a charitable heart. They just don't want it coming out of *their* pockets."[6]

Riley commented after the defeat—"I'm tired of Alabama being first in things that are bad, and last in things that are good."[7]

The comment made by the leader opposing Riley could be said about more than just Alabamians. "Alabamians have a charitable heart, but they just don't want it coming out of *their* pockets." We like the *idea* of mercy and charity—we just don't always like the *action* if it involves sacrifice on our part. But mercy is as mercy does.

Nathan Hale was a left-handed pitcher throwing in the low 90s with an opportunity to pitch at the highest level of collegiate athletics—that is, until elbow problems and arm surgeries unraveled his baseball dreams. In the wake of his disappointment, he discovered another dream along the way—a dream of God for the impoverished of the world. Years later, Nathan and his friends have purchased 2.5 acres of land next to a massive garbage dump in Honduras where children rummage for food daily. On that land a sizable garden is being planted that one day will yield an annual harvest of one million pounds of food to feed thousands of Honduran children foraging garbage dumps for food.[8] Blessed are the merciful.

AN INVITATION TO HEALING—NOT JUST OTHERS BUT OUR OWN

The merciful will be shown mercy. The possibilities are limitless in terms of how God may show it to them. In the wake of suddenly losing their fifteen-year-old son, Jantsen, to an undetected heart defect, Randy and Pam Cope began to receive monetary gifts in his memory. They established a memorial fund in his name. More than $25,000 was given to it though the Copes had little idea as to what to do with it. Were they to build playgrounds in their hometown or buy soccer uniforms for the local school? After some time of deliberation they decided to help fund an orphanage in Vietnam that their friends had started. To ensure that this was the best place for Jantsen's money, Randy, Pam, and their daughter Crista (eleven at the time) traveled to Vietnam to visit the orphanage. The Copes had never seen poverty before like what they saw in Vietnam. As they walked the streets of Saigon and Da Nang, they began to pay attention to, and eventually get to know, some of the children forced to live and beg on the streets. After returning home, Pam continued to seek understanding about the problem of street children in Vietnam, commonly known as *bui doi*, or "dust of the earth"—the beatings and fear they were forced to endure, their hunger and malnutrition, the probability of some being picked up by child traffickers and forced to work in hard labor conditions or sexual bondage.

Randy and Pam sought to do their part to try and save the few children that they could from a dark future. Partnering with volunteers in Vietnam, Jantsen's gift was used to rent a house in Saigon, hire house parents, and bring in 15 children who would have a permanent home, an education, medical care, and an opportunity to be a part of a family. Months later, they rented another house, took in 15 more children, and "Touch a Life" was born. Today, Touch a Life supports 211 children in eleven group homes throughout Vietnam and has now expanded into Ghana, West Africa, where 68 children have been rescued from child trafficking and now have a place to call home, along with an education and medical care.[9]

Our family has the privilege of a friendship with the Copes. They would be the first to tell you that, while they are irrevocably scarred by the sudden loss of their precious son, there is a measure of healing to be found in being a conduit for the mercy of God in the lives of others. Loving mercy can be healing because God is found in the mercy. In Isaiah, God confronts the people for losing sight of mercy in the way they were going about their lives. They were a people rich in religious ritual, disciplined in their observance of the religious calendar, and yet genuinely befuddled over a sense of disconnectedness from their Creator. Then God begins to shed some light on their sense of disconnectedness:

> "Is not this the kind of fasting I have chosen:
> to loose the chains of injustice
>   and untie the cords of the yoke,
> to set the oppressed free
>   and break every yoke?
> Is it not to share your food with the hungry
>   and to provide the poor wanderer with shelter—
> when you see the naked, to clothe them,
>   and not to turn away from your own flesh and blood?
> *Then your light will break forth like the dawn,*
>   *and your healing will quickly appear"* (Isaiah 58:6–8, emphasis added).

It could very well be that the opportunities for us to extend mercy in our world aren't just invitations for us to help. They could be invitations to our healing as well. God delights in mercy. He lives in it. Blessed are the merciful, for they will be shown mercy.

*"Blessed are the
pure in heart, for
they will see God."
(Matthew 5:8)*

HEARTS WIDE OPEN

For earth to become heaven, for life to truly be good, Jesus says that one must tend to the deep places of the heart.

The human heart is a strong, muscular pump slightly larger than a fist. The engine of the human body pumps blood continuously through the circulatory system. Each day the average heart expands and contracts—what we commonly refer to as a beat—100,000 times and pumps about 2,000 gallons of blood. In a seventy-year lifetime, an average human heart beats more than 2.5 billion times. Of course, if you eat cream-filled doughnuts every day, the number increases.

The circulatory system is a network of elastic tubes carrying blood throughout the body. It includes the heart, lungs, arteries, arterioles (small arteries), and capillaries (very tiny blood vessels). These blood vessels carry oxygen and nutrient-rich blood to all parts of the body. If all the small veins that carry oxygen and nutrient-depleted blood back to the heart and lungs were laid end-to-end, they'd extend about 60,000 miles. That's enough to encircle the earth more than twice; one could drive from Los Angeles to New York City twenty-two times in that distance. Or, one could drive from Nashville to Detroit, round-trip, sixty times.

Circulating blood brings oxygen and nutrients to all the body's organs and tissues, including the heart itself. It also picks up waste products from the body's cells. These waste products are removed as they are filtered through the kidneys, liver, and lungs.

Blood flow returns through veins from the entire body into the inferior and superior vena cava that lead into the right atrium of the heart. Blood is then pumped into the right ventricle and out to the lungs. From the lungs it enters the left atrium and is pumped into the left ventricle, then out through the ascending and descending aorta to the rest of the body. Even more amazing is the fact that blood flow is actually different *in utero* (where it bypasses the lungs) then changes when babies are born.

Dr. Bill Frist knows the genius of the human heart and the mysterious workings of that heart that simply can't be explained. Frist is a leading heart surgeon in America. He knows the routine. He usually gets a call in the middle of the night. There's a heart waiting in a body that won't live if it's taken off of life support. Someone has graciously signed to be a donor. The call comes in: "Dr. Frist, we have a heart that needs to be transplanted." Frist has done this several times. The doctor wakes up, dresses, and travels as fast as he can to the nearest hospital where he'll take a helicopter to the patient on life support. He takes an Igloo cooler with him.

Frist arrives at the hospital in Louisville, Cincinnati, or Atlanta. The donor waits. The heart pumps only because of the power of life support. Frist knows he has four hours to get the beating heart into a waiting patient. The Igloo cooler is opened. He packs the heart in dry ice. Back to Vanderbilt Medical Center in Nashville. The recipient, whose life is about to change forever, is prepared. The surgeons and nurses go to work. Then there's a moment, everything's in place, nothing is happening. The warm blood begins to flow. The heart is cold, frozen for almost four hours. But once the blood from the recipient flows into it, something happens. A miracle in the mundane.

No one can explain exactly what happens. Warm blood flows. The heart remembers what it was created to do. One twitch. Two twitches. No flat line. A beat. New life. All because the heart has the unexplainable ability to remember what it was created to do.

THE SPIRITUAL HEART

I'm surprised Jesus didn't say, "Blessed are those with brilliance of mind or courage of the soul." Instead, Jesus says "Blessed are the pure in heart, for they will see God." What the heart does for the physical body, apparently, the heart also does for the spiritual body. The heart is the center of all life, physical and spiritual. What the physical heart is to the human body, the spiritual heart (center) is to the life of following God.

Methodist pastor James Howell writes, "For Jesus, as for all people in Bible times, the 'heart' was not a pulsating organ inside your chest to be strengthened by exercise and a good diet or cured by the cardiologist's tool kit. The heart is your true self. The heart is the part of you that feels, delights, grieves, desires. The heart is the 'imagination,' the place inside where we conceive, where we make connections, where we dream. The heart is the place where you exercise your freedom, where you decide, the mechanism that chooses what to do this evening, whom you will marry, whether to lie or not, how to respond to a crisis. The heart is the sphere where we meet God, or avoid meeting God."[1]

The heart is the spiritual center of a person's being. It is neither inherently good nor bad. Rather, the heart is the battlefield for the grace of God and the lies of Satan to wage war for our affection and allegiance. The heart is a mixture of divinity (we are fashioned in God's DNA) and sin.

The Bible has a great deal to say about the human heart. Genesis depicts the darkness of the human heart (6:5; 8:21) by describing humanity as people with hearts turned toward evil all the time. When Abraham learns that he will have a son when he should be playing shuffleboard in Panama City, he laughs deep in his heart (Genesis 17:17). Shechem sexually violates Dinah (Genesis 34) "and his heart was drawn to Dinah" (verse 4). When Joseph's brothers believe they are on their way to death row, Scripture says their "hearts sank"—they were moved in the deepest place humanly possible (Genesis 42:28). God's great nemesis in Exodus is Pharaoh, whose heart is hardened in order for God to accomplish liberation and justice (see Exodus 7:13 and other verses in Exodus 7—11).

The psalmist has much to say about the human heart. One writer claims that God saves those whose hearts are pure (7:10) while another reminds the reader that only a fool would deny God in his or her heart (14:1–3). Psalm 37:4, one of my favorite psalms, reminds us that if we revel in God's character and presence, God will gift us with all the things that reside in our heart. In one of David's most important hours, he pleads with God to give him a steadfast spirit and a pure heart (51:10). A writer in Proverbs, in one of the more honest moments of the book, makes claim that the purposes of the human heart are *deep waters* (Proverbs 20:5, emphasis added). That is, as humans, we are complex, divided beings, equally capable of angelic majesty and animal debauchery. In Ezekiel 36:26, God tells his people that a heart transplant is about to take place: "I will give you a new heart and put a new spirit in you; I will remove from you your heart of stone and give you a heart of flesh."

Jesus mentions the heart several times in the Gospel narratives (*kardia* is the basis for our English word *cardio*). In addition to the beatitude under consideration, he directly refers to the human heart ten additional times in the Gospel of Matthew.[2] In almost every text in Matthew, Jesus assumes that the heart is the center of one's life. That is, everything else in one's life flows from what is in the heart. In 22:37–40, Jesus says that the entirety of Torah is summed up in loving God (and others) with all of one's heart, soul, and mind (see Deuteronomy 6:5). Here, as in other places, Jesus leads with the heart. Jesus believes, as one author notes, "that inward roots are directly connected to outward fruits" (Matthew 7:15–21; 15:11).[3]

At the beginning of the Sermon on the Mount, Jesus' invitation to imagine the Good Life, he says these simple words.

Blessed

are

the

pure

in

heart,

for

they

will

see

God.

Jesus told a parable that puts flesh on this concept of the pure at heart seeing God. He says two men went to the Temple to pray. One was a religious scholar, the other a member of Hell's Angels. The religious scholar prayed, "God, thanks for making me a great servant in your work. Thanks for allowing me the chance to pray this public prayer and that I am not like this biker." Meanwhile, the biker goes to one knee, weeping, "God, I'm messed up. I got nothing." Jesus says that two men went to the Temple to pray and worship. One man, the Hell's Angel guy, went home forgiven. The other man just went home (see Luke 18:9–14).

What we call innocence today might just be what Jesus meant by "purity of heart."

Special needs children reflect purity of heart that can only be explained by the power and creative genius of God. Maybe my translation speaks to your heart: *Blessed are those who've been gifted by God to innocence.* We are always living from our heart. Blessed are those who have a singular focus and an undiluted passion for God.

Purity of heart is to will the love of God into one's life. It is to love God with an undiluted, unadulterated, uncompromising passion above all other things and people.

One of my heroes in preaching was the father of a girl with Down syndrome. Megan was the light of their family's life. On one occasion at an early age, Megan got into some dog food and had it all over her mouth and lower face. My friend came into the backyard and found his daughter. Not offering affection on a regular basis, Megan looked at her father, and said, "Kiss, Daddy? Kiss, Daddy?" Mike hesitated for a moment and then simply went for it, dog food and all.

Two reminders strike me as I write this. First, people with handicaps often resemble the heart of Jesus more than allegedly "normal" people. Second, the relationship between parents and a handicapped child is a fair parallel to the relationship between God and his church.

On another occasion, my friend spent the entire day with his daughter. While they were playing in the back yard, all of a sudden, Megan sprinted toward the house. "Where are you going?" Mike asked. No answer. He followed her into the house, through the kitchen, into the master bathroom in her parents' bedroom. Megan grabbed her mother's toothbrush, walked over to the toilet and began swishing it around, laughing. That night, while getting ready for bed, Mike read a book, and waited for Diane to come in. As she began to brush her teeth, Mike couldn't keep his composure—he burst out laughing.

"What? What's so funny?"

"Nothing."

"What's so funny?"

"Well, I . . . you see . . . I caught Megan using your toothbrush to clean the toilet this morning." Silence ensued. Diane fired back.

"Whose toothbrush do you think she uses all the days you are at work?"

The father of this brilliant young girl also shared this story in a personal note:

Two days before Megan died, another special friend of Megan's came in to see her. He asked if he could have a minute alone. . . .

It wasn't until much later that I learned that Alan had asked to see Megan alone because he had been carrying a secret for many, many years. Something he felt he could tell no other human being.

So for the first time in his life, in the presence of pure love in human flesh, he shared the deepest secret of his life. When he told me about it, he said that he still trembled as he remembered the look of understanding and love in her eyes.

Just an hour before Megan took her last breath, the oldest man in our church came into her pediatric ICU room to say "good-bye." He actually stretched the truth a wee bit to get in, telling the nurses that he was her great-grandfather. In an extended, metaphorical sense, that was true.

He walked into our holy space, placed a hand on her head, raised the other hand, looked up, and said, "May the gates of heaven open wide to receive this sweet child." His words are carved into my memory.

Here was the perspective of one who loved so much, who knew that death isn't final, who understood that a well-lived life was coming to an end. His final act of friendship was a great-grandfatherly blessing just before Megan died.[4]

Blessed are the pure in heart, for they will see God. And when we see them we see a glimpse of God. Blessed are those who have a purity—an undiluted, unadulterated love of God.

While struggling financially in my first year of marriage to Kara (we were both finishing degrees), I signed up to work for Metro Public Nashville Schools as a substitute teacher. All of the pranks I'd played in time in the public school systems of Metro Detroit would come back to haunt. My favorite assignment while working for MNPS was the experience of working with children with special needs. I'll never forget the time we took a group of middle school students from Antioch to the Adventure Science Center in the city. Somehow, two girls I was responsible for went missing and I sprinted all over, in a panic, trying to find them. Calling their names, sweat pouring down my face, I panicked. After about thirty minutes, I came around a corner and found both girls sitting calmly in a corner playing a game with one of the volunteers from the center.

"Big Boy," one of them shouted. The volunteer, a young woman in her mid-twenties, looked at me strangely. "Big Boy, Big Boy, Big Boy!" they both yelled. I was embarrassed but I knew what they were saying. Their nickname for me was Big Boy because I'm 6'4". Not what you want to be called in public by two middle school girls.

The volunteer broke the awkward silence, "They've been repeating Big Boy over and over. I guess they were expecting you. Glad you could make it." Over the course of my life, I never received as many hugs from any group of people in my life as I did working with special needs children at MNPS.

Blessed are the pure in heart, for they will see God. And we will in turn see God in them.

A young girl with Down syndrome teaches us how to kiss and laugh. Other special needs children remind us about the power of touch. Dorothy, hardly a child, but still a child, holds her friends as God did when God walked among us in Jesus. All of them reflect Jesus' words that the pure in heart are the ones who can see God. Maybe you and I, the got-it-all-together-impressive-folk, are the ones with special needs. Of course, I'm not suggesting that the only people who are pure in heart are people with disabilities. I am suggesting, however, that if you don't know what "pure in heart" looks like, those who are disabled are the best and first place to begin looking for what Jesus meant.

God is among those who possess purity of heart. Run to them. Run as fast as you can. For in running to them, you usually end up running into the heart of Jesus.

*"Blessed are the peacemakers,
for they will be called
children of God."
(Matthew 5:9)*

THE ROAD TO PEACE

Peacemaking is the intentional decision to participate in God's future (the shalom of God) in the present. Peacemaking often shows up in counterintuitive ways. Peacemaking is radical trust in the absurdity of God and the cross over the certainty of power, violence, and revenge. Theologian Donald Hagner writes, "In the context of the beatitudes, the point would seem to be directed against the Zealots, the Jewish revolutionaries who hoped through violence to bring the kingdom of God. Such means would have been a continual temptation for the downtrodden and oppressed who longed for the kingdom. The Zealots by their militarism hoped furthermore to demonstrate that that were loyal 'sons of God.' But Jesus announces . . . it is the peacemakers who will be called 'children of God.' "[1]

The difficulty believing Hagner lies in how you answer this question: Do you begin reading the story of God in Scripture in Genesis 1 or Genesis 3? That is, do you read the story, and your own life, through the lens of the power, creativity, goodness, and imagination of God (Genesis 1) or do you read the story through the lens of sin, chaos, rebellion, violence, and death (Genesis 3)?

If you read the story starting from the wrong place, you might end up in the wrong place.

Because the essence of Christianity is this—it's not so much that Jesus is like God, the scandal of Christian faith lies in the belief that *God is like Jesus*. If it cannot be said of Jesus, it can no longer (if it ever could have been in the first place) be said of God. Paul states it like this, "[Jesus] is the image of the invisible God" (Colossians 1:15). The writer of Hebrews captures this truth: "[Jesus is the] reflection of God's glory and the exact imprint of God's very being, and he sustains all things by his powerful word" (Hebrews 1:3 NRSV).

Part of the purpose of Jesus' life is to show us what it looks like to live the life God intended us to live. One of the most difficult elements of living the heaven-on-earth life is to imagine what Jesus meant when he named peacemakers as children of God—the only people in his beatitude litany who receive such respect and affection.

Jewish and Christian theologians commonly recognize the belief that Genesis 1 and 2 describe the peace of God or the shalom of God.

Furthermore, many Jewish theologians today note that so much of Torah is concerned with helping humanity reclaim the good and whole relationship—the shalom of God—as experienced in the very beginning of the story.

Theologian Cornelius Plantinga, describes the shalom of God as "the webbing together of God, humans, and all creation in justice, fulfillment, and delight is what the Hebrew prophets call shalom. We call it peace, but it means far more than mere peace of mind or a cease-fire between enemies. In the Bible, shalom means *universal flourishing, wholeness and delight*—a rich state of affairs in which natural needs are satisfied and natural gifts fruitfully employed, a state of affairs that inspires joyful wonder as its Creator and Savior opens doors and welcomes the creatures in whom he delights. Shalom, in other words, is the way things ought to be."[2]

Shalom and peace mean . . .

To make amends.

To make good.

To be (or to make) peace.

To restore.

Completeness.

Wholeness.

Peace.

Wellness.

Prosperity.

Wellness.

Many of us think peace is no more than the absence of conflict. In Jewish teaching, shalom is much bigger. It's an imaginative exercise of epic proportion.[3]

Isaiah 65:17–25 is perhaps the strongest Old Testament embodiment of the coming of the shalom (peace) of God.

"See, I will create
　new heavens and a new earth.
The former things will not be remembered,
　nor will they come to mind.
But be glad and rejoice forever
　in what I will create,
for I will create Jerusalem to be a delight
　and its people a joy.
I will rejoice over Jerusalem
　and take delight in my people;
the sound of weeping and of crying
　will be heard in it no more.

"Never again will there be in it
　an infant who lives but a few days,
　or an old man who does not live out his years;
the one who dies at a hundred
　will be thought a mere child;
the one who fails to reach a hundred
　will be considered accursed.
They will build houses and dwell in them;
　they will plant vineyards and eat their fruit.

No longer will they build houses and others live in them,

    or plant and others eat.

For as the days of a tree,

    so will be the days of my people;

my chosen ones will long enjoy

    the work of their hands.

They will not labor in vain,

    nor will they bear children doomed to misfortune;

for they will be a people blessed by the LORD,

    they and their descendants with them.

Before they call I will answer;

    while they are still speaking I will hear.

The wolf and the lamb will feed together,

    and the lion will eat straw like the ox,

    and dust will be the serpent's food.

They will neither harm nor destroy

    on all my holy mountain,"

                         says the LORD.

Therefore, one of the key aims of Jesus—often lost on modern-day audiences—was to show Israel the path to co-creating the shalom of God in their present circumstances. His way of doing this, the kingdom of God, often came into sharp conflict with the Jewish and Roman authorities of the day. Peacemaking was at the heart of all that Jesus was attempting to set in motion.

The shalom of God is a constant theme in the New Testament, where key Scriptures like Revelation 21—22 and Romans 8 all describe and invite the shalom of God.[4] In fact, peace is the common greeting in most of the New Testament letters.[5]

Jesus captures the Jewish passion for peace and shalom, and the remaining pages of New Testament must be interpreted through this vision.

Therefore, in this beatitude, blessed are the peacemakers, Jesus provides a foreshadow of his own destiny. His life following this beatitude becomes a public parable of that which he's already expressed in the teaching. His life is the meaning of the beatitude.

New Testament scholar Charles Campbell points out that Jesus' triumphal entry into Jerusalem, in Matthew 21:1–11, is street theater. Jesus is performing a *Saturday Night Live* parody of the ways in which Herod and Caesar strolled into cities they controlled through power and violence. Jesus is literally playing the fool in order to suggest a different way of leading and loving; peacemaking in the here and now. "The whole time, however he is turning the world's notions of power, rule, and kingship on their head. His theater is a wonderful piece of political satire. . . . The event takes on the air of a carnival, where those on the bottom of society festively unmask and challenge the dominant social order."[6] Campbell goes on to argue that "Blessed are the peacemakers" becomes a living word that animates the entire Sermon on the Mount. In this new community, this new way of being human, Jesus dares his listeners to imagine a world that appears to be foolish.[7]

The question is this: do we really think Jesus knew what he was talking about? Can we really pursue peace in a violent world? What would it look like if we did?

The Gospel of Matthew—the larger Jesus-Story—doesn't leave us to wonder. All throughout the first Gospel, the writer gives us clear snapshots of Jesus embodying what he meant in this beatitude.

If you want to know what Jesus meant when he said that "peacemakers are children of God," watch how he lived. Matthew's larger story lays this out in easy-to-follow fashion: Jesus' birth is a threat to the Roman government, which keeps "the peace" through violence and bullying (1:18—2:23). Fast-forward to his time in the wilderness; here Jesus refuses the tactics of Satan, showing he will be a suffering king, not a king who needs power to rule (4:1–11; 20:17–28). Then Jesus begins to teach his disciples that his suffering will become their suffering (10:16–23). That is, commitment to peacemaking isn't just for Jesus, it's for anyone bold enough to wear his name and proclaim his kingdom project.

Matthew's Gospel also gives us a glimpse of a minor but important character, John the Baptist, as a faithful sufferer committed to Jesus' peacemaking project (14:1–12). Jesus again reiterates the necessity of suffering on behalf of others, peacemaking for a purpose (16:21–28; 17:22–23). Instead of wishing revenge or pain against someone who's wronged you, Jesus encourages his disciples to practice peacemaking through reconciliation (18:15–35).

The entire Passion narrative—the willingness of Jesus to suffer as a means to peace—should be considered Jesus' ultimate commitment to showing the truth of the beatitude that peacemaking is what God's children do. The kingdom and the cross can't be separated (Matthew 26—28). It is in this setting that Jesus says, after one of his own disciples attempts to answer violence with violence: "Put your sword back in its place, . . . for all who draw the sword will die by the sword" (26:52).

"The crucified God stands in judgment upon the kings, the corporations, the nations, the emperors, the rulers, the presidents, the prime ministers of this world who seek violently to wield power, to control and dominate."[8] Jesus demonstrates the true path to peace.

Jesus' kingdom project was an extension of the peace project of Torah and the prophets. This is why *peace* is such a prominent word and concept in the flow of the New Testament.

Peacemaking is central to almost every single narrative/text in Scripture.[9]

The careful reader of Matthew's Jesus-Story often asks this question: If Jesus' mission in announcing the kingdom of God is to somehow participate in the Jewish belief in the shalom of God, why did Jesus clearly state, in Matthew, that he did not come to "bring peace to the earth" but that he came to bring, not peace, "but a sword" (10:34)? Read in context, the answer is clear: Jesus is addressing the human propensity to be comfortable, to play it safe, to avoid taking a risk (compare Matthew 25:14–30). The gospel message is dangerous. It's countercultural. It might even cost you your life. For anyone to play Matthew 10:34

as a trump card, ignoring the numerous passages previously mentioned, is irresponsible at best.

If anyone desires to know what Jesus meant when he said "Blessed are the peacemakers, for they will be called children of God," all we have to do is watch how Jesus lived. Because how he lived is what he meant.

CHARLIE STROBEL, PEACEMAKER

Peacemaking is the intentional decision to participate in God's future (the *shalom* of God) in the present. This peacemaking often shows up in counterintuitive ways. Peacemaking is radical trust in the absurdity of God—the cross and the certainty of power—violence and revenge.

Jesus was a peacemaker extraordinaire and he invites his disciples to take up the same script, improvising the peaceful way in creative fashion.

All of this was academic and intellectual for me until one of my mentors, Father Charlie Strobel, shared one of the most painful experiences of his life with me.

This is peacemaking with a face.

Charlie Strobel grew up in the heart of downtown Nashville (in an area now known as Germantown).[10] He was born into a devout Christian family with deep roots in the Catholic Church. Charlie's father who, because of an accident at a young age, suffered from a physical handicap his entire life. Charlie was just four years young when his father, Mutt Strobel, died. His mother brought the children together, encouraging them with these words: "God will take care of us, and your father will watch over us, and we have to stay together." From an early age, Charlie was baptized into the truth of the human experience: life is full of so much joy and pain; life and death; community and loneliness. Charlie's mother, Mary Catherine, refused to wallow in her tough luck—she had four young children (and two aging aunts!) to feed and care for. She went to work right away serving, for twenty-nine years, the Nashville Fire Department until her retirement. In addition to working, caring for her young and vulnerable family, Mary Catherine exhibited a heart for the "least of these" in Nashville's growing city. Mary Catherine looked out for the poor and homeless with simple, daily gestures of kindness and generosity.

As Charlie grew older he felt the call of God on his life to enter into ministry. I'm told through interviews and conversations with co-workers that though he would later become a priest, his first love was professional baseball. Somehow, God kept calling him to come closer for the dream God had put in Charlie's heart.

Two memories shaped the particulars of God's calling on Charlie's life to enter into ministry. First, he recognized that he couldn't go to school with black neighborhood friends like Tony. Second, a black man had converted a barn-like structure, near his home, into a two-room shack for his family. This man got up at dawn each morning to work his day job delivering coal; after supper at home, he left again and worked as a janitor until midnight. "He did this six days a week but was never able to make enough money to get out of that place and buy a real house. When I grew up and heard people say that the poor were lazy and didn't want to work, that was not my experience, my frame of reference, at all."

After winning an award for Nashvillian of the year, Strobel, commented, "All of our stories are there, in the Scriptures. If you can locate yourself there, you're in great company, you're not alone, other people have been there. It's all about God. We are the story, and God is the plot."

After a few detours for graduate school and ministry, Charlie ended up back in Nashville as priest for East Nashville's Holy Name Catholic Church. "When I came to Holy Name in 1977, we didn't *see* 'homeless people,' but there were poor people . . . we would make them peanut butter and jelly sandwiches." In the early 1980s homelessness began to increase in cities all over the US. Nashville was no exception. By 1985, Strobel's passion for the poor and vulnerable in the city began a program that would forever change the city of Nashville through Room in the Inn ministries.[11]

However, tragedy would strike the Strobel family once more. On December 9, while making volunteer rounds, Mary Catherine Strobel went missing; two days later, her body was discovered in the trunk of her car. A man who had escaped from a prison psychiatric unit was later charged in her murder and the murders of several other people.

Can you see Charlie?—a man who barely knew his father, who remained celibate because of his calling as a priest—now grieving over the closest representation to God in his life: the death of his mother. (For many of us that would have been the death of God.)

When the Strobel family first learned of their mother's tragic death, they issued this statement to the media: "Today our family is grieving deeply over the death of our mother. This terrible event in our lives points out for us how heartless our world can be. But our mother spent her whole life working to change that. . . . She loved people of all races, especially the poor, and was our inspiration." Upon learning that the police had arrested a suspect thought to have been the person who murdered Mary Catherine, the family reminded the city of Nashville: "The cruelty of her death, as devastating as it is, does not diminish our belief that God's forgiveness and love, as our mother showed, is the only response to the violence we know."

William Scott Day was tried and found guilty of the death of Mary Catherine as well as six other people. Even still, Charlie Strobel and the rest of the immediate family stayed true to their convictions that God, through Jesus, was calling them be reconciled. "We claim no higher authority than Jesus and make no greater appeal than his words (referring to the Sermon on the Mount). I can think of no way that his execution would bring satisfaction. I hope that ages from now our family descendants will look back at our actions and understand that in an age of vengeance, we chose not to be vengeful but tried to be faithful to our most cherished family teaching, namely, that God is love itself, and has given us his love generously, yes, even unto death, and expects nothing less from us. . . . In my mind, William Scott Day is a child of God, created in the image of God, loved by God. Can we think of him in any other way? In the destiny of God, he is forever linked to us and has become part of us and we a part of him."

I know of no finer example of Jesus' words than that we are to seek peace and reconciliation with those whom we harbor anger, bitterness, and hate. If for no other reason, the person you are setting free when you reconcile is yourself.

Upon his mother's death, Strobel noted two lessons his mother left him. First, God was going to help the family, momma would watch over them. Second, great needs still exist all around and the family should respond with every ounce of love they could summon.

Today, because of Charlie's passion and vision, along with the support of hundreds of Nashvillians, Room in the Inn is one of the most holistic, comprehensive centers of hospitality for the poor and lonely in Nashville. Room in the Inn works with close to two hundred congregations in Nashville, housing two hundred fifty men, women, and children per night, and has been copied in thirteen other US cities. "A man with no children who's been a father to thousands." A man who once said, "We are the only species who knows that we will die, that everything else will go on but that our time on earth is short. So, what do you do with that time?"

Father Strobel demonstrates the power of the Jesus Way. While it is not easy, it is not impossible. Blessed is Charlie Strobel, for he is a peacemaker and he is a child of God.

IT DOESN'T HAVE TO BE LIKE THIS

Have you ever noticed what happens in Genesis with the sibling narratives? The younger brother always supplants/overthrows the elder brother. In a culture based in honor and shame, land rights, and family authority, this would be hard to swallow for listeners and readers.

Cain kills Abel.

Isaac, the younger brother, and Ishmael live in noticeable tension because they know their family story.

Jacob, the younger brother, steals Esau's birthright. Eventually they reconcile.

Joseph is sold into slavery by his older brothers. He rises to power through incredible circumstances and has the chance to crush his brothers; instead he welcomes them with hospitality and undeserved love.

And Exodus joins the fun. Exodus begins with a story about a younger brother Moses and his older siblings, Aaron and Miriam. The elder brother is a supporter of Moses—God's reluctant mouthpiece.[12] The elder brother will see God's purposes unfold. And because God loves to keep us sharp, he also reminds us that the siblings in the family aren't just boys. Miriam is part of the plot too.

It's like Genesis and Exodus—and eventually Jesus in bodily form—are saying that there is often tension between family members/communities/religious sects, but that doesn't mean it has to be this way. Living in a grace-soaked state is possible. It requires imagination, humility and hard work. But just because something is hard doesn't mean it's impossible. Especially if you believe that in your baptism you've been gifted with the presence of the Spirit. Charlie Strobel is a living embodiment of this story. Anger. Animosity. Bitterness. Rage. Violence. Pain.

I tried all this theology out on my friend Jonathan. You know, *peace, shalom*, the whole big picture of *restoration and hope*. Jonathan reminded me of how God came to Abraham and told him to leave his family, how God would make Abraham into a great nation, they would be a blessing to the whole world . . . that when God spoke those words the world only thought cyclically. The Greeks would have said "what goes around comes around," while the Mesopotamians would say "it's all folly" or "the apple doesn't fall far from the tree." But when God came to Abraham it was, perhaps, the first time in human history that someone would have heard, "It doesn't have to be this way."

This was the gift of the Jews.

It doesn't have to be this way.

Jesus offers us a way out of these vicious cycles.

Jesus became what we are so we could become what he is. Jesus wanted us to live as peacemakers, not as Cain and Abel.

Blessed are the peacemakers, for they will be called children of God. Jesus believed this so strongly that he would rather die for his enemies than send them to hell.

And die he did.

Because the teaching wasn't just a teaching.

The teaching became his life.

And the teaching can become your life too.

Heaven can be yours on earth.

CHAPTER 9

> *"Blessed are those who are
> persecuted because of righteousness,
> for theirs is the kingdom of heaven."*
> *(Matthew 5:10)*

TRUE GRIT

Brennan Manning once lamented that too many spiritual leaders operate as travel agents passing out brochures and speaking of destinations that they themselves have never visited.[1] When it comes to reflecting on Jesus' words concerning persecution, I could very well be considered one of "those" leaders. There is no shortage of other leaders, though, whose lives help us grasp Jesus' startling words about persecution.

The story of Said Musa captivated many in America in the first few months of 2011. The forty-five-year-old father of six lived in his native Afghanistan. He grew up Muslim before deciding to become a follower of Jesus as an adult. In May, 2010, Said was arrested and imprisoned in the wake of participating in a service in which other Afghans were being baptized into Christ. He was told by Afghan authorities that he would be hanged in February 2011 unless he formally renounced Christ and returned to Islam. Said refused, his saga becoming news in America when the State Department began to get involved and the American media picked up the story. A groundswell of interest and prayer emerged on behalf of Said. By the end of February 2011, Said was released by authorities.

Many Christ-followers throughout the world are under fire for their faith, and there is so much to be said to the American church about the importance of praying for the persecuted global church. The writer of Hebrews urges us to "continue to remember those in prison as if you were together with them in prison, and those who are mistreated as if you yourselves were suffering" (13:3). While losing one's life or being threatened with the loss of life because of one's faith is the greatest form of persecution, it's not the only form. Jesus went on to expound upon the eighth and final beatitude: "Blessed are you when people insult you, persecute you and falsely say all kinds of evil against you because of me" (Matthew 5:11). Words can be powerful and Jesus acknowledges that the tongue can be a powerful instrument of persecution. His crucifixion wouldn't be the first time he was persecuted though it was the most violent expression of his persecution. Whether the fires and swords of persecution are literal or lingual, it's important for any disciple to be prepared to face resistance along the way.

If we were to think of the Beatitudes as rungs on a ladder, then the eighth beatitude reminds us that the ladder leans against a cross. Living in light of the realities Jesus articulates in the previous seven beatitudes will most surely guarantee personal experience with the eighth beatitude.

CERTIFICATES OF AUTHENTICITY

Jesus is not saying his disciples should seek persecution. After all, persecution will find them. Neither is Jesus sanctifying or glorifying all persecution. Sometimes believers are persecuted *not* because of something having to do with kingdom-righteousness, but instead because of their own self-righteousness, or rudeness, or pettiness. The apostle Peter wrote:

> If you suffer, it should not be as a murderer, or thief or any other kind of criminal, or even as a meddler. However, if you suffer as a Christian, do not be ashamed, but praise God that you bear that name (1 Peter 4:15–16).

Not all persecution is related to the righteousness of the kingdom, but the righteousness of the kingdom will invite persecution. Toward the end of his life, the apostle Paul affirmed to Timothy, "Everyone who wants to live a godly life . . . will be persecuted" (2 Timothy 3:12). Persecution faced as a result of embodying the values of the kingdom of heaven is one of a Christ-follower's certificates of authenticity[2]—a sign that the kingdom of heaven is "settling in" upon the follower. Perhaps this is at the heart of George MacLeod's lament, "The greatest criticism of the Church today is that no one wants to persecute it because there is nothing very much to persecute it about."[3] Jesus would later say to his disciples:

> "This is the verdict: Light has come into the world, but people loved dark-
> ness instead of light because their deeds were evil. Everyone who does evil
> hates the light" (John 3:19–20). "If the world hates you, keep in mind that it
> hated me first. If you belonged to the world, it would love you as its own. As
> it is, you do not belong to the world. . . . That is why the world hates you.
> Remember what I told you: 'A servant is not greater than his master.' If they
> persecuted me, they will persecute you also" (John 15:18–20).

Perhaps these words of Jesus were echoing in Peter's mind when he wrote, "If you are insulted because of the name of Christ, you are blessed, for the Spirit of glory and of God rests on you" (1 Peter 4:14). This conviction could explain the seemingly strange response of the early church to persecution, such as in Acts 5 after Peter and some of the apostles were persecuted by the Sanhedrin: "The apostles left the Sanhedrin, rejoicing because they had been counted worthy of suffering disgrace for the Name" (Acts 5:41). Counted worthy. They considered persecution a backhanded compliment in the sense that the religious establishment had decided they, and what they stood for, were of consequence—a force be reckoned with—"worth" dealing with. Jesus would later liken his followers to salt and light (Matthew 5:14–16)—two things that have an impact on their surroundings, whether food or dark-ness. Their presence brings change to an environment unless they are removed. Persecution is an acknowledgment that a difference-maker is on the scene and must be dealt with if people don't want anything to be different.

Early on the morning of May 1, 1685, John Graham of Claverhouse arrived with a group of soldiers at the home of John Brown, a young Scottish minister. Brown had been accused of not supporting the King of England as the supreme authority over the church. Graham had come to confront Brown and give him an opportunity to repent of his conviction. When Brown refused, citing Jesus as the supreme head of the church, Graham flew into a rage telling him to prepare to die. Brown turned to his wife Isabel, who was witnessing the confrontation, and said, "You see me summoned to appear, in a few minutes, before the court of heaven, as a witness in our Redeemer's cause, against the Ruler of Scotland. Are you willing that I should part from you?"

Isabel replied, "Heartily willing." Graham ordered six of the soldiers to fire at Brown, but none of them did. Instead, they stood there, virtually motionless. Graham drew his own pistol and fired a shot into Brown's head.

Turning to Isabel, Graham asked, "What thinkest thou of thy husband now, woman?"

The young widow replied through her shock and tears, "I have always thought well of him, but never more than now."[4] As far as Isabel was concerned, there was no greater certificate of her husband's authenticity than his execution for the sake of Christ. Sooner or later, ambassadors of the kingdom of heaven will have opportunity to suffer on behalf of the King who himself suffered on behalf of everyone. Jesus brings two things to mind in the course of providing perspective for those being persecuted.

FOR THE JOY SET BEFORE US

In Matthew 5:12, Jesus extends his commentary on the eighth beatitude, "Rejoice and be glad, because great is your reward in heaven." In the face of persecution, Jesus calls the one being persecuted to recognize eternal realities that lay ahead. While the Beatitudes have so much to say about realities and implications of the kingdom of heaven on this side of the grave, they are not void of addressing the kingdom's realities and implications on the other side of the grave. It's worth noting that Jesus himself "walked his talk" when it came to his own persecution. The writer of Hebrews said it was "for the joy set before him he endured the cross, scorning its shame, and sat down at the right hand of God" (12:2). Jesus would later say in the Gospel of Mark:

> "Truly I tell you . . . no one who has left home or brothers or sisters or mother or father or children or fields for me and the gospel will fail to receive a hundred times as much in this present age: homes, brothers, sisters, mothers, children and fields—along with persecutions—and in the age to come eternal life" (Mark 10:29–30).

The apostle Paul reflected with the Corinthians upon his own experience with persecution:

Therefore we do not lose heart. Though outwardly we are wasting away, yet inwardly we are being renewed day by day. For our light and momentary troubles are achieving for us an eternal glory that far outweighs them all. So we fix our eyes not on what is seen, but on what is unseen, since what is seen is temporary, but what is unseen is eternal (2 Corinthians 4:16–18).

Keeping in mind the end of the story is of profound value when it comes to weathering the plot twists along the way. Focusing on eternal realities has everything to do with being faithful in the midst of persecution, because a disciple who is unattached to the temporary can be hard to intimidate. But if we're too attached to our body, our possessions, our reputation, our money, our career, our agenda, the margin is wide for us to be intimidated by persecution when it threatens to impact any of those things. The most dangerous believers in the world to the kingdom of darkness are the ones who live as though they have nothing to lose. In the course of being scrutinized by his apartheid government's Eloff Commission, Bishop Desmond Tutu said:

There is nothing the government can do to me that will stop me from being involved in what I believe God wants me to do. I do not do it because I like doing it. I do it because I am under what I believe to be the influence of God's hand. I cannot help it. When I see injustice, I cannot keep quiet, for, as Jeremiah says, when I try to keep quiet, God's Word burns like a fire in my breast. But what is it that they can ultimately do? The most awful thing that they can do is to kill me, and death is not the worst thing that could happen to a Christian.[5]

It's difficult to intimidate disciples who are so focused on eternal realities. From Jesus, to Paul, to John Brown, to Desmond Tutu, to Said Musa—the line of those who have been persecuted for the sake of righteousness is long. But the line didn't begin with Jesus.

A GREAT CROWD BEHIND US

Jesus continues to extend the eighth beatitude in Matthew 5:12, "for in the same way they persecuted the prophets who were before you." Jesus had a profound sense of consciousness about those in the Old Testament who were persecuted as a result of righteousness. On one occasion he described the entire witness of the Old Testament, from the first book to the last book, as a record of "righteous blood that has been shed on earth, from the blood of righteous Abel to the blood of Zechariah" (Matthew 23:35).[6] It's easy to feel alone when being persecuted. Our cosmic enemy would love for us to believe we are alone, but the witness of Scripture begs to differ. There is a "great cloud of witnesses" (Hebrews 12:1) with which we can find company.

One of the reasons one might feel alone when under the gun of persecution has something to do with who is often holding the gun on the other end—those who themselves are "religious." Have you considered who the "they" are that Jesus is referring to when he says, "for in the same way *they* persecuted the prophets who were before you" (Matthew 5:12, emphasis added)? It was often God's own people who persecuted their own prophets with Jesus being the ultimate example of this—being put to death by the religious leaders of his own people in a cooperative effort with Rome.

So often the most painful persecution a follower of Christ faces is persecution from the "inside." At times there are philosophies, ideologies, theologies, and practicalities within organized Christianity itself that will be occasionally challenged by the implications of Jesus' teaching concerning the kingdom of heaven and the blessedness of where God is at work. As a result, persecution can often be an "inside job." Consider Martin Luther and his work that helped to bring about the Reformation as we know it. He suffered greatly at the hands of other believers. Consider the Caucasian preachers who stood by the side of Martin Luther King, Jr. during the Civil Rights Movement and yet were ostracized (and worse) by many in their own churches.

Jesus warned his disciples, "All this I have told you so that you will not fall away. They will put you out of the synagogue; in fact, the time is coming when anyone who kills you will think they are offering a service to God" (John 16:1–2). Perhaps in this way, more than any other, followers share in the suffering of Christ. He bears the scars of persecution at the hands of his own people.

FELLOWSHIP OF THE SCARS

It's no small thing that the resurrected body of Jesus bore scars. Though it had been transformed and clothed in power, it, nevertheless, bore the marks of suffering in his time on earth. This is a gift to his followers for so many reasons, one of which is that those who are persecuted for righteousness may be continually reminded they are not alone. There is a fellowship to be found with the scars of Jesus who suffered at the hands of "religion," the "religious," and, in the end, the world. Peter, writing to a community of persecuted believers, called their attention to the One who suffered ahead of them:

> If you suffer for doing good and you endure it, this is commendable before God. To this you were called, because Christ suffered for you, leaving you an example, that you should follow in his steps.
>
> "He committed no sin,
>
> and no deceit was found in his mouth."
>
> When they hurled their insults at him, he did not retaliate; when he suffered, he made no threats. Instead, *he entrusted himself to him who judges justly*" (1 Peter 2:20–23, emphasis added).

It's easier to entrust ourselves to one if we know he has been where we are. Knowing he walked in our shoes makes all the difference in the world in us continuing to follow in his steps when we are persecuted because of righteousness.

THE END OF OURSELVES (AGAIN)

In persecution there are newfound opportunities to be brought to the end of ourselves and experience the supernatural sustainment of God. *The Message* translates Matthew 5:10 in this way, "You're blessed when your commitment to God provokes persecution. The persecution drives you even deeper into God's kingdom." It could be said that Jesus himself experienced this reality in Gethsemane on the eve of his crucifixion as he wrestled with the implications of the will of his Father for his own life. An angel appeared from heaven and strengthened him (Luke 22:43). At the beginning of his second letter to the Corinthians, Paul reflected on a recent season of persecution in his life:

> We do not want you to be uninformed, brothers and sisters, about the troubles we experienced in the province of Asia. We were under great pressure, far beyond our ability to endure, so that we despaired of life itself. Indeed, we felt we had received the sentence of death. But this happened that we might not rely on ourselves but on God, who raises the dead (2 Corinthians 1:8–9).

One has to wonder if this isn't why, over the course of history, some of the greatest movements of kingdom righteousness have occurred in seasons of tremendous opposition and persecution. In the midst of such adversity and persecution, the participants in the righteousness of the kingdom are brought to the end of themselves and to a radical reliance upon God for everything. Serbian bishop Nikolai Velimirovic spoke out against Nazism in the early 1940s and was arrested and taken to the Dachau concentration camp. Out of his experience, Velimirovic penned this prayer:

> Bless my enemies, O Lord. . . . Enemies have driven me into your embrace more than friends have. Friends have bound me to earth; enemies

have loosed me from earth and have demolished all my aspirations in the world. . . .

Just as a hunted animal finds safer shelter than an unhunted animal does, so have I, persecuted by enemies, found the safest sanctuary, having ensconced myself beneath your tabernacle, where neither friends nor enemies can slay my soul.

Bless my enemies, O Lord.[7]

Velimirovic's prayer is one that reflects the experience of persecution driving him beyond the end of himself and into the sanctuary of God. But to read this prayer is also to see the authenticity of Velimirovic's faith.

The other day I was in a home and saw some fruit in a basket in the middle of a kitchen table. Instinctively, I reached for an apple and drew it to my mouth to bite into it when I realized it wasn't real—it was designer fruit. These days the designer fruit that people use to accentuate their homes can look so much like the real thing. In many cases, it's difficult to know what's real and what's not until you handle it or even cut into it. The same can be said when it comes to persecution in one's life. It's in the midst of persecution—when a person is handled, even cut into—that a person may be truly revealed for who or what they really are on the inside. Is this not what happened with Jesus at the cross? It was on the cross we saw just how merciful he really was—just how pure and single-mindedly focused on the will of God he really was—just how committed he really was to making peace between God and all of us. It was on the cross he was cut into, and the world witnessed that he bled what he taught.

Those who follow in the footsteps of Jesus will be persecuted because of righteousness. And when they are there will be One who will fellowship with them as they participate in his sufferings—One who will remind them, through the scars on his resurrected body, that there will be life beyond the wounds of persecution. The worst things will not be final things. Blessed are those who are persecuted because of righteousness, for theirs is the kingdom of heaven.

MAKE SOMETHING HAPPEN

"You are the salt of the earth.
But if the salt loses its saltiness,
how can it be made salty again?
It is no longer good for anything,
except to be thrown out and trampled
underfoot. You are the light of the world.
A town built on a hill cannot be hidden. Neither
do people light a lamp and put it under a
bowl. Instead, they put it on its stand, and it
gives light to everyone in the house. In the
same way, let your light shine before others, that
they may see your good deeds and
glorify your Father in heaven."
(Matthew 5:13–14)

A few years ago, I had the privilege of spending a couple of days at the Paris, Texas, ranch of legendary football coach Gene Stallings. One day, with Coach Stallings's permission, I rummaged around his attic—a wonderland for an avid football fan, brimming over with mementos from decades of coaching national champions on the college level and Super Bowl champions on the professional level. While there I stumbled across items from his playing and coaching days under another towering figure in the history of coaches—Paul "Bear" Bryant. Among my favorite stories about Bryant concerns a simple sign he posted at the exit of the locker room, under which his Alabama Crimson Tide team walked on their way out to the field—"Make Something

Happen." Such a caption would be fitting for Jesus' association of his followers with salt and light. In doing so, Jesus was very much recognizing their capacity to make something happen. The proper response to the blessings Jesus had just proclaimed in the Beatitudes was not lofty reflection. It's action—action rooted in and shaped by the realities of which the Beatitudes speak.

The Beatitudes provide the context for understanding what Jesus is really saying in likening his followers to salt and light. In the Beatitudes Jesus is announcing what it means for the world that the kingdom of heaven is near. It's going to make a difference for the poor in spirit, those who are mourning, the meek, those who hunger and thirst for righteousness, the merciful, those pure in heart, peacemakers, and those who are persecuted because of righteousness. In every case, his declaration begins with "blessed" to indicate that these are the arenas where God is working—where his reign will make a difference. The Beatitudes help us realize what God is doing, what God values, where God's at work, and invite us to align our lives accordingly.

As we align our lives with the realities mentioned in the Beatitudes we become as salt and light in the world, but we are only salt and light to the degree that we align our lives with such realities. To put it another way, we are only as salty and enlightening in our world to the degree that we reflect the nature of the King and his kingdom as described in the Beatitudes.

LIFE-PRESERVERS

We have trouble appreciating what Jesus is saying in likening his followers to salt because of the way we use and see salt today. It gets more than its share of bad press in our country for the role it plays in a variety of illnesses and maladies such as high blood pressure. Many people are on low-sodium diets and counting the milligrams of salt in their food. There's even a prejudice against salt being on the table in higher-end restaurants or in people's homes. Have you ever been on the receiving end of a quasi-dirty look from a host when you asked someone to pass the salt, with your request being taken as a personal indictment of their dish not being seasoned well?

Today salt is cheap and accessible, but that wasn't true in the ancient world. Good salt was difficult to come by and was of great importance because salt was best known as a preservative. Salt was used to keep food from rapidly decaying and going bad. When fresh foods became scarce, salted foods were integral to having sustenance for a season. Salt's capacity to act as a preservative is most likely the story behind "salt" serving as a symbol of the covenant between God and His people in the Old Testament. It was a "covenant of salt."[1] God's people of the Old Testament understood God's covenant and instruction would preserve their lives.

In calling his followers the salt of the earth, Jesus is, in essence, calling them the life-preservers and decay-preventers of the world. As one comforts the mourning, or hungers and thirsts for things to be made right, or shows mercy, or participates in peacemaking, so they are being salt. While there's plenty of evidence of followers of Christ doing more harm than good in our world, there's also plenty of evidence of the impact they have had, for the better, when they embodied the realities conveyed in the Beatitudes.

In the nineteenth century, William Wilberforce (in England) and John Woolman (in America) sought to preserve life through their abolitionist work—they sought to end slavery in the name of Jesus Christ.[2] Their efforts were an expression of hungering and thirsting for things to be made right in our world. In the twentieth century another follower of Christ, Desmond Tutu, led an initiative of mercy and reconciliation after the abolition of apartheid. He was appointed chairman of the South African Commission for Truth and Reconciliation, which provided an environment for victims to share their stories publicly while former perpetrators of oppression and violence could come forward, take responsibility for their actions, and ask for forgiveness and amnesty. While the process was messy and far from perfect, remarkable expressions of peacemaking emerged with far fewer displays of vengeance and bloodshed than were feared.[3] It would be surprising to some today to find out that followers of Christ, who were embodying values represented in the Beatitudes, are buried in the history of organizational movements involving orphan care, adoption agencies, and the humane and compassionate treatment of the mentally ill. But then again, isn't that consistent with the nature of salt? When someone has a really good meal, they don't talk about how great the salt is. It's buried in the meal. But if salt's missing, one can taste the difference.

Igbo-Ora is a sleepy little farming community in southwest Nigeria that lays claim to a mysterious wonder in the fertility world. The majority of families in its region have at least one set of twins. Today, fertility experts and researchers are studying Igbo-Ora in an effort to understand the miracle of fertility so that they might help others throughout the world who struggle with infertility.

What makes the story of Igbo-Ora so remarkable is that a little more than a century ago it was a community that would be considered one of the most unlikely places on earth to find a set of twins—alive. A century ago, in the tribal culture of Nigeria, people believed twins were an evil omen—a potential sign of the mother having been with two men at the time of their conception. In many cases, women and their twins were killed on the day of delivery.

Mary Slessor, a Scottish missionary, is credited with putting an end to such a practice. She came to the region of Nigeria and spent her life ministering to the physical and spiritual needs of the people, leading villages to Christ and educating them as to what Scripture said about the blessing of children. Through her steady and faithful proclamation of the gospel of Jesus, the execution of twins and their mothers ceased. Today, a place once known for the death of twins is now known as "the land of twins." Buried in the history of Igbo-Ora is some salt named Mary Slessor who hungered and thirsted for things to be made right on behalf of newborns, as well as the culture's understanding of blessings and curses.[4]

There are so many ways the salt of the kingdom of heaven has been making a difference in our world, and yet there remain all kinds of ways our world is suffering from not enough salt—or light for that matter.

ILLUMINATORS

It's difficult for us to grasp what a commodity light was in the days of Jesus. In twenty-first-century America our nighttimes, particularly in the more populated areas, are illuminated in so many ways with the glowing signs of fast-food restaurants, gas stations, theaters, stadiums, street lights, parking lots, and security lights. Living amidst our urban sprawl makes us so accustomed to lights at night that it's difficult to appreciate how dark it can get in the middle of nowhere, particularly on a cloudy night. In the ancient world, there weren't many options for light beyond the sun, the moon, oil lamp, or candlelight.

Living in North Texas, we have more than our share of violent thunderstorms and tornadoes every spring. A few years ago, one of those massive storm systems rolled through our region like a freight train in the middle of the night. It shook the house and knocked out our power. It was pitch black. Our boys were startled and began crying in the darkness as my wife and I were in a mad scramble to find a flashlight. Of course, every one we stumbled upon had dead batteries. The crying escalated along with the running into furniture and walls. Finally, Tara managed to find a candle and some matches. It was amazing what one candle did to light up a room and calm down three anxious little boys—well, four if you count me. It wasn't until I had stumbled around in a house in the middle of the night, in the midst of a massive Texas thunderstorm, that I realized just how precious light is.

In referring to his followers as the light of the world, Jesus was making a profound affirmation of the significance of their lives, particularly when their lives are distinguished by the kinds of values and deeds consistent with Jesus' declarations in the Beatitudes. "A town built on a hill cannot be hidden." In Jesus' day towns would be built on hills and along cliffs in order to defend themselves from attacks. Jerusalem was built upon the higher elevations in the area for this reason. Jesus' followers knew what it was to see towns built on hills and how easy it was to spot one from miles away. It was impossible to hide a town built on a hill.

On occasion, we'll hear a well-intentioned believer say something along the lines of, "Well, we just need to let our light shine"—when the truth is, light shines. There's little need to focus on *letting* our light shine. It just *does*. "A town built on a hill cannot be hidden." When the Beatitudes are fleshed-out in the life of believers in the midst of the world, their lives will shine and "the light will come on" for many in the midst of darkness. When we turn on a light in a room, we don't turn it on so that we can look at it, we turn it on so that something else can be seen in the light. Jesus acknowledged that people will see and praise God in light of the good deeds of his followers, specifically deeds embodying the spirit of the kingdom proclamations made in the Beatitudes.

HALTING THE ECLIPSE

There is some measure of thought in our world that those who profess to follow Jesus have ceased to be very salty or enlightening. It could very well be that the salt and light needing to be restored in the witness of Christ's followers has everything to do with a return to living the good life envisioned within the Beatitudes.

It's always been curious to me that though Jesus referred to himself as the light of the world (John 8:12) he also referred to his followers in the same way. So which is it? Perhaps the relationship between the sun, the moon, and our world could be of help. The moon is a source of light for people of the world at night. But its light is not its own. It functions as a reflector of the sun's light. Apart from the sun, the moon cannot shine. Every once in a while we observe what's known as a lunar eclipse, when the earth is aligned directly in between the sun and the moon, thus blocking the sun's light upon the moon and, hence, eclipsing the moon. The moon ceases to be lighted and has no light to reflect upon the earth. This could very much be the picture for many professed followers of Jesus today. Our role is to shine amidst the darkness. The light is not our own, but his. We can only reflect the light of the Son to the degree we are in his light. So often, though, much of what is fallen about our world comes in between us as followers and the Son. Values, philosophies, and ways of functioning—far removed from those of the kingdom of God—begin to overshadow our lives. They eclipse us and render us void of light to shine amidst the darkness.

GRAB THE CHALK

When it comes to being the light, the first and greatest step we as followers can take is to come into the light ourselves—to heed the words of Jesus, "Repent, for the kingdom of heaven has come near" (Matthew 4:17). Sound familiar? We've come full circle—ending where we began—with Jesus' declaration of the kingdom of heaven coming near. The Beatitudes show us the way of repentance that leads to salty and enlightening lives—lives that make a difference.

One of the great revivalists of the late nineteenth and early twentieth centuries was Rodney "Gypsy" Smith. He was once asked by a young pastor how he could help bring about a revival at his church. Smith told him to go home, grab a piece of chalk, draw a circle on the floor, kneel within the circle, and then pray for revival for everyone on the inside of that circle. After that, he would start to see revival on the outside of the circle.[5] There's much to be said for starting on the inside of the circle and stepping into the light of the realities Jesus spoke of in the Beatitudes. In a world that has its share of religious institutions and leaders that act as though they have a monopoly on God, the good life Jesus invites us into is found through him having a monopoly on us.

It's time to put a halt to the eclipse.

Grab the chalk.

Heaven on earth awaits us—and the rest of the world through us.

It makes a difference.

THE COLOR OF WATER

If you and I are anything alike, you sometimes experience a disconcerting or even sick feeling after reading a book on Jesus, discipleship, and the kingdom of God. That is, right now you might have a gut reaction, "But I'm not even sure I believe any of this is true: *God becoming a prophet in Nazareth, miracles, divinity, dying for sin, resurrection.*" If you are a person who believes, as do I, that faith is not the absence of doubt but rather action in the face of doubt, then these closing words are for you.

Or, you might be thinking, "This all sounds so inspiring and even compelling, but there's no way I can actually live up to Jesus' vision of the kingdom of heaven." This is for you, too.

Ten years ago, James McBride wrote a memoir that captured the hearts of many Americans. The book, *The Color of Water*, is a tribute to McBride's mother who raised twelve children on her own in the Red Hook Housing Projects in Harlem, New York City. As a boy James knew his mother was different. But when he asked about it, she'd simply reply, "I'm light-skinned." Later he wondered if he was different, too, and asked his mother if he was black or white. "You're a human being," she snapped.

On another occasion, after a rousing experience in church, James asked his mother if God was white or black. "God is a spirit . . . neither. God is the color of water."

James's biological father, a devout Christian who started the Brown Memorial Baptist Church in Harlem that still stands today, died while his mother carried James in her womb. At the age of fourteen, James's stepfather died. The death of two husbands sent his mother into a state of panic, uncertainty, fear, and general chaos. When I was fourteen I was worried about going to the middle school dance. McBride wondered if he'd ever have a father.

McBride's mother coped by riding her bike all over Harlem. While most drove cars, took the bus, hopped on the subway, she decided to ride her red bike through the busy streets of America's biggest city. "The image of her riding that bicycle typified her whole existence to me. Her oddness, her complete nonaware-ness of what the world thought of her, a nonchalance in the face of what I perceived to be imminent danger from blacks and whites who disliked her for being a white person in a black world. She saw none of it."[1]

The Color of Water is the story of his mother's life—the story of a rabbi's daughter (she was Jewish but later became a devout Christian because of the acceptance she experienced in a black Christian community), born in Poland, raised in the south, abused by the men in her life, only to escape to New York City to make a new life for herself and her children. In the end, all twelve of her children attended college: they became doctors, lawyers, teachers, and psychologists. From the projects to Harvard, their mother's eccentric ways and unrelenting love pushed them to seize all that life offered. In retrospect, all of her children realized that their mother's love was like the power of the moon. "It's what made the river flow, the ocean swell, and the tide rise, but it was a silent power, intractable, indomitable, and thus completely ignorable."[2]

There's a question in the reader's mind in the *The Color of Water*: What is nature of this person, this caregiver, life giver, supporter, relentless, sacrificing, and caring challenger? It's this question that readers of the Beatitudes, of Jesus' Sermon on the Mount, must wrestle with. It's an ultimate question, upon which everything is built, our success, our understanding, our belief in that "intractable, indomitable" power. The question is this: Is Yahweh a good parent? This is the question running underneath each story of the Old Testament, and the question that Jesus answers in defining the kingdom of God: heaven on earth.

As we read Scripture, we see that God understands that as the child grows, the child must learn to learn to walk and to grow without the constant attention of the parent. Why would we dare follow these provocative teachings if we don't trust God?

The answer might surprise you:

It is in attempting to live in the imagination of Jesus (on display in the Beatitudes) that we obtain the trust in God we seek.

It is in doing that we believe more deeply.

It is in risking that we become more confident in Jesus' brilliance.

In the sacred truths of the Beatitudes, we are introduced to both the nearness and distance of God. Because God is a parent, God loves. God comes close. But God also wants us to become the humans God created us to be and distance allows us to grow. Distance gives us space to become who we already are in God's eyes.

My oldest son, Lucas, started school for the first time recently. My wife and I knew, intellectually, that the best thing for him was to be away from his parents for a time—to have distance. Only by being with others, in new settings, can he find out if everything we've been teaching him is true and good. He has to jump. He has to fly. He has to have his own life.

So it is with God. Because a truly loving parent knows when to be near and when to have separation. The separation, the training, can be tough. It's not easy. But just because something isn't easy doesn't mean it's impossible.

God is our parent. Sometimes God feels near. Sometimes God feels far. But God is in the midst of all of it.

The Beatitudes keep us connected to God, even when we don't "feel like loving God" or we don't "feel God's closeness." They are a compass that keeps us oriented to reality.

One of the great challenges of following Jesus in our culture is to make sure that the Jesus we are following is not a Jesus we've created in our own image. That is, it's one thing to follow a Jesus who ends up looking like you, rather than the Jesus recorded in the Gospel accounts of the New Testament.

Jesus' words in the Beatitudes are simply an invitation to believe that God's world is more real than anything else, that God is a near, merciful, just parent.

That God is worthy of trust, that God has our best interest in mind. The Beatitudes teach us that God is more for us than we are for ourselves.

Faith is about seeing the world as God sees it. Not simply seeing the world for what it is—in all its paradox of beauty and death—but also seeing the world for what it will one day become.

That's the beginning of heaven invading earth.

Through you. Through us.

Heaven's coming crashing into earth. Can you see it?

The kingdom's coming. Heaven's coming to earth.

Move. Act. Take a risk.

Live as if it's true.

NOTES AND REFERENCES

CHAPTER 1

1. "Ask Fred," by Fred Smith, *Leadership Journal*, Summer 2005, 40.
2. Isaiah 9:1–7, 9:11; 24:14–23:12; 26; 31:1—32:20; 33; 35; 40:1–11; 42:1—44:8; 49; 51:1—52:12; 52:13—53:12; 54; 56; 60; 61; 62.
3. Glen H. Stassen, *Living the Sermon on the Mount: A Practical Hope for Grace and Deliverance* (San Francisco: Jossey-Bass, 2006), 25.
4. Warren Carter, *Matthew and the Margins: A Sociopolitical and Religious Reading* (Maryknoll, NY: Orbis, 2000), 131.
5. Frederick Buechner, *The Clown in the Belfry* (San Francisco: Harper, 1992), 152–153.

CHAPTER 2

1. Mark McMinn, *Why Sin Matters* (Tyndale, 2004), 69–71.
2. *Living the Sermon on the Mount*, 39.

CHAPTER 3

1. http://marginalrevolution.com/marginalrevolution/2004/09/the_crying_bar.html
2. Nicolas Wolterstorff, *Lament for a Son* (Grand Rapids: Eerdmans, 1987), 85-86.
3. Reflex tears and emotional tears differ in their levels of protein. Emotional tears have much

more protein than reflex tears. This is common knowledge in scientific and medicinal communities. For an example, see http://www.biosyntrx.com/articles.php?id=753 or do a basic Google search of reflex and emotional tears.

4. Barbara Brown Taylor, *An Altar in the World: A Geography of Faith* (San Francisco: HarperOne, 2010), 49–50.

5. Philip Yancey, *What Good Is God?* (Nashville: Faith Words, 2010), 206–208. Yancey also notes that although the Middle East is the birthplace of Christianity, only 2 percent of Palestinians are Christian. As recently as half a century ago, Palestine boasted a 40 percent Christian population. The United States' most recent war with Iraq has chased out half of the 1.4 million Christians formerly living there. Yancey calls this place "an oasis of beauty in a desert of poverty."

6. Ibid., 207–208.

CHAPTER 4

1. *Living the Sermon on the Mount*, 48.

2. Christina Kelly (editor of *Elle Girl, YM, Jane*, and *Sassy*, in a confessional article about the process of the female magazine industry), quoted in Timothy Keller, *The King's Cross: The Story of the World in the Life of Jesus* (New York: Dutton Publishing, 2011), 78–79.

3. From a lecture Dr. Carl Sagan delivered at Cornell University on October 13, 1994.

4. From Augustine's third sermon on the Sermon on the Mount, quoted in Jim Forest, *The Ladder of the Beatitudes* (Orbis Books, 1999), 59.

5. Ibid., 56.

CHAPTER 5

1. Quotations and other material on pages 50–52 are from Malcolm X, *The Autobiography of Malcolm X* (New York: Grove Press, 1964), 9–37.

2. See Josh's book, *The Feast*, for a fuller exposition of Malcolm X's story and the prophetic edge of Scripture (pp. 57–66). Josh Graves, *The Feast: How to Serve Jesus in a Famished World* (Abilene, Texas: Leafwood Publishers, 2009).

3. Cornel West, American philosopher, activist, and author.

4. Richard Lischer, *The Preacher King: Martin Luther King Jr. and the Word that Moved America* (New York: Oxford Press, 1995), 181. Lischer's entire section on prophets and Martin Luther King's prophetic role in America is outstanding (see pp. 173–194).

5. See also Exodus 5:1, Leviticus 19:33–34; Psalm 37:12; Isaiah 42; Matthew 21:32; Acts 17:31; Romans 6:18. Matthew, here are some key verses to consider: 1:9; 3:15; 5:10; 5:20; 6:1; 6:33; 21:32. In 2 Timothy 3:16, while describing the genius and power of Scripture, Paul says that Scripture's purpose is to prepare people to live like Jesus, to be trained in righteousness.

6. The King James Bible translates Psalm 23:3 as "He leadeth me in the paths of righteousness"; the New International Version reads, "He guides me along the right paths"; and the Douay-Rheims Bible translates it this way: "He hath led me on the paths of justice."

7. I (Josh) have an entire chapter dedicated to this in *The Feast*, 141–153.

8. N .T. Wright, *Simply Christian: Why Christianity Makes Sense* (HarperOne, 2010), 9. Wright continues by pointing out, that, while Islam and Judaism are different than Orthodox Christianity, each religion's sacred text reveals a yearning for cosmic justice.

CHAPTER 6

1. Warren Carter, *Matthew and the Margins: A Sociopolitical and Religious Reading* (T&T Clark, 2005), 134.

2. For a more comprehensive discussion concerning mercy in the Greco-Roman context, see B. F. Harris "The Idea of Mercy and Its Greco-Roman Context"; in *God Who Is Rich in Mercy*, ed. by P. T. O'Brien and D. G. Peterson (Homebush: Lancer Books, 1986), 89–105.

3. Consider the examples found in Deuteronomy 24 and Leviticus 25

4. Judith Warner, "The Charitable-Giving Divide," *New York Times Magazine*, August 20, 2010, 11.

5. "Wins & Losses," by Warren Cole Smith, *World*, October 2010, 11.

6. *Living the Sermon on the Mount*, 55.

7. Ibid.

8. Thanks to Dr. David Fleer for the story of Nathan Hale and the Honduran garden. Adapted from his sermon "Blessed Are the Merciful" February 6, 2011 at the Otter Creek Church in Nashville. See www.ottercreek.org for the sermon podcast page.

9. For more on Randy and Pam Cope's story, check out Pam Cope's memoir *Jantsen's Gift: A True Story of Grief, Rescue, and Grace* (Grand Central Publishing, 2011); also, touchalifekids.org.

CHAPTER 7

1. James Howell, *The Beatitudes for Today* (Louisville, KY: Westminster John Knox Press, 2006), 68.

2. Matthew 5:28; 6:21; 9:4; 11:29; 12:34; 13:15; 15:8; 15:18, 19; 22:37. See also Romans 1:21; Philippians 4:7; Revelation 2:23. Rembrandt painted a scene from the story of the prodigal son (Luke 15) of the father embracing his son. One preacher I know says that the Rembrandt painting depicts the son burying his head in his father's chest because, "the son wants to listen to the heartbeat of his father." As the father's heart beats for his son, so God's heart beats for the world. (*The Return of the Prodigal Son* is an oil painting from about 1667.)

3. It's important to note that when our hearts are divided, it generally relates to two things: 1) seeking the approval of others (Matthew 6:1–18) or worry connected to money and material possessions (6:19–34). The former and the latter can't be separated!

4. See Mike Cope, *Megan's Secrets: What My Mentally Disabled Daughter Taught Me About Life* (Abilene, TX: Leafwood Publishers, 2011), 200, 14–15, 94–95.

CHAPTER 8

1. Donald Hagner, *Word Biblical Commentary*, Vol. 33a, *Matthew 1–13* (Dallas: Word Publishing, 1993), 92.

2. Cornelius Plantinga, Jr. *Not the Way It's Supposed to Be: A Breviary of Sin* (Grand Rapids, MI: Eerdmans, 1995), 9–10.

3. Jesus viewed the world through the lens of Genesis 1 and 2. Much of his kingdom mission was to usher in an age that faithfully reflected the world described in Genesis 1 and 2. It is not too much of a stretch to suggest that Genesis was the gospel Jesus read and lived by. Genesis was the script that funded Jesus' imagination. Jesus believed in the authority (Genesis 1:2), power (1:1–3), reativity/imagination of God (1—2). Jesus also believed in Genesis' fundamentally radical claims concerning the goodness of creation (1:4, 10, 12, 18, 21, 25, 31) and the divinity that every human bears (1:26ff). How else, for instance, could Jesus offer the two pillar teachings of the good Samaritan (Luke 10) and the prodigal son (Luke 15) if not for the latter?

4. See also: Luke 2:14; John 14:27, 20:19; Acts 10:36; Romans 16:20; and Revelation 6:4.

5. Romans 1:7; Colossians 1:2; 1 Corinthians 1:3; 2 Corinthians 1:2; Ephesians 1:2; Philippians 1:2; 1 Thessalonians 1:1; Titus 1:4; 1 Peter 1:2; 2 Peter 1:2; 2 John 1:3; Jude 1:2; Revelation 1:4.

6. Charles Campbell's "The Folly of the Sermon on the Mount" in *Preaching the Sermon on the Mount: The World It Imagines* (Fleer and Bland, eds), (St. Louis, MO: Chalice Press, 2007), 60.

7. Reconciliation is more important than vengeance (Matthew 5:21–26); women are no longer treated as objects (5:27–32); enemies are loved not destroyed (5:38–48); religious practices are not about superiority (6:1–18); desire for wealth is not the prime motivation in life (6:19–34).

8. Lee Camp, *Mere Discipleship: Radical Christianity in a Rebellious World* (Grand Rapids: Brazos Press, 2008), 106.

9. A few more examples: Romans 14:19 "Let us therefore make every effort to what leads to peace and mutual edification"; Hebrews 12:14 "Make every effort to live in peace with everyone . . ."; In the middle of a teaching on the powers and principalities, Paul refers to gospel as the "gospel of peace" in Ephesians 6:15; James 3:18 "Peacemakers who sow in peace reap a harvest of righteousness"; 1 Peter 3:11 "They must turn from evil and do good; they must seek peace and pursue it."

10. All details through page 99 are from my (Josh's) conversations with Charlie Strobel.

11. www.roomintheinn.org

12. Exodus 7:7. Aaron is three years older than Moses. My friend, Doug Sanders pointed this out to me.

CHAPTER 9

1. See Brennan Manning, *The Ragamuffin Gospel: Good News for the Bedraggled, Beat-Up, and Burnt Out* (Multnomah Books, 2005).

2. Persecution is not the only "certificate of authenticity." For instance, the Spirit (Romans 8:9) and the fruit thereof (Galatians 5:22) testify to authenticity.

3. George F. MacLeod, *Leadership*, Vol. 2, no. 4.

4. There are two sources for this story. Jack Deere, *Surprised by the Voice of God* (Grand Rapids, MI: Zondervan, 1996), 76–77. Deere modernized the spelling and grammar in the quotations as well as removed the Scottish-isms. Also, John Howie, ed. William McGavin, *Scots Worthies* (Glasgow: W.R. McPhun, 1846; orig. ed., 1775), 443–446.

5. Richard H. Schmidt, *Glorious Companions: Five Centuries of Anglican Spirituality* (Grand Rapids, MI: Eerdmans, 2002), 328.

6. Books in the Hebrew Testament are in a different order than Christian Bibles. The first book is Genesis (containing the story of Abel) and the last book is Zechariah (the Zechariah who would be martyred). Jesus' point being the Hebrew Scriptures (Old Testament), from beginning to end, bear witness of people being persecuted for righteousness.

7. http://www.orthodoxytoday.org/articles/VelimirovichBlessEnemies.php (accessed 9/29/2012).

CHAPTER 10

1. See Leviticus 2:13; Numbers 18:19; 2 Chronicles 13:5.

2. For a more comprehensive summary of this, see Rodney Stark, *For the Glory of God: How Monotheism Led to Reformations, Science, Witch-Hunts, and the End of Slavery* (Princeton: Princeton University Press, 2004), 338–353.

3. See "South Africa: Breaking Down the Walls," by Philip Yancey, in *What Good Is God: In Search of a Faith That Matters* (New York: FaithWords, 2010), 143–168. Also, "The Church Is

Responsible for So Much Injustice," by Tim Keller, *The Reason for God: Belief in an Age of Skepticism* (New York: Dutton, 2008), 63.

    4. Janet and Geoff Benge, *Mary Slessor: Forward Into Calabar* (Seattle: YWAM, 1999).

    5. http://bereanbibleheritage.org/extraordinary/smith_rodney.php (accessed 9/29/2012).

EPILOGUE

    1. James McBride, *The Color of Water* (Riverhead Trade, 2006), 7–8.

    2. Ibid., 94.

IN APPRECIATION

From Josh: Kara, Lucas, and Finn are the relational center of my life. I adore them, love them, and know, deep in my bones, that they are the home God created me to love. Otter Creek Church (www. ottercreek.org) has been gracious to let me think and dream out loud concerning the Jesus I'm writing about in this book. The shepherds and ministers of Otter Creek Church embody so much of what I'm writing. Lee Camp opened up my imagination to the power of Jesus' upside-down kingdom in ways I'm still learning to appreciate. My literary agent, Wes Yoder, has been a terrific conversation partner and encourager along this journey. The Graves family, Josh Ross, Jonathan Storment, Sara Barton, Phillip Camp, David Rubio, Randy Harris, Mike Cope, John Barton, Patrick Mead, Randal Wilcher, Ken

Switzer, Doug Sanders, Scot McKnight, Rubel Shelly, David Fleer, John York, and Brad Crisler are significant theological conversation partners in my life. All of them contributed to this book. I value their insight second only to their friendship. The entire Abingdon Team, most notably Lil Copan, was exceptional to work alongside. Lauren Winner, writer and editor *par excellence*, pushed us to write a better book. I hope we listened.

From Chris: Tara, for twenty years I've drunk deeply of the good life alongside her and through her. Skyler, Garrison, and Cooper—the trio of young men who have my heart wrapped up inside of them and walking around. Rick Atchley—no one has modeled for me more, week-in and week-out, the integrity, discipline, and excellence in faithfully proclaiming the reign of God. Reg Cox—my first mentor who conveyed to me the primacy of the message of the kingdom of God and set the pace for me in pursuing God; Doug and Kimberly Conder, Sheila Seidman—for your faithfulness to labor and love through the ministry of intercession; Kim Seidman—my sister and a trusted conversation partner; the elders and staff of The Branch—what a thrill to serve alongside you for the last twelve years. Lauren Winner, Wes Yoder, Lil Copan, and the entire Abingdon team.

We are dedicating this book to our sons—Skyler, Garrison, Cooper (Chris's trio), Lucas, and Finn (Josh's duo) because we hope our sons come to know and love the most important human who's ever lived: Jesus of Nazareth. He never traveled outside of a region larger than the state of New Jersey and yet, here we are, two thousand years later, telling his stories, singing his songs, and embracing his passion for things to be on earth as they are in heaven.

Grace and Peace,

Chris and Josh
Pentecost 2012

Dr. Josh Graves is the teaching minister for the Otter Creek Church in Nashville, Tennessee, (www.ottercreek.org). Josh focused his doctoral studies on the relationship of faith, culture, and postmodernism at Columbia Seminary. He enjoys teaching at conferences and churches around the US. Josh's first book, *The Feast* (Leafwood, 2009), explored the North American missional church conversation in *memoirish* fasion. You can read his blog/resource site: www.joshuagraves.com or follow him on twitter: @joshgraves. When Josh isn't playing pick-up basketball, he loves being with his wife (Kara), and two sons (Lucas and Finn).

Chris Seidman lives in Coppell, Texas, with his wife, Tara and their three boys, Skyler, Garrison, and Cooper. Since 2001, he has served as senior minister of The Branch (www.thebranch.org)—a multi-site church in Dallas. He has also written *Little Buddy: What a Rookie Father Learned About God From the Birth of His Sons* and *Before Stones Become Bread*. Chris is privileged to speak and teach in churches and conferences across the country and agonizes on the golf course weekly. You can follow Chris on twitter: @chrisseidman.